THEY WERE NAKED

The Language of Marital Unity

THEY WERE NAKED

NANA-SEI TWERETWIE

MAPLE
PUBLISHERS

They Were Naked:
The Language of Marital Unity

© 2025 by Rev. Nana-Sei Tweretwie

All rights reserved. No part of this book may be reproduced or transmitted in any form or by any means, electronic or mechanical, including photocopying, recording, or by any information storage and retrieval system, without prior written permission of the author and/or publisher, except where permitted by law.

ISBN 978-1-83538-893-8 (Paperback)
     978-1-83538-894-5 (E-Book)

Contact the Author via:
tweretwienana70@gmail.com

PUBLISHED BY
Maple Publishers
Fairbourne Drive, Atterbury,
Milton Keynes,
MK10 9RG, UK
www.maplepublishers.com

DEDICATION

I dedicate this book to the glory of God, whose grace and wisdom have guided every word written within these pages. To Jesus Christ, the source of all wisdom, knowledge and truth, whose love and sacrifice have been the foundation of my faith and inspiration. I also dedicate this work to the Holy Spirit, who has given me strength, in-depth understanding, many revelations, and the power to accomplish this glorious work. Again, to those seeking a deeper relationship with the Lord, especially the Body of Christ, and those who are ordained for eternal life yet have not received the Lord. I pray that these words of wisdom lead you closer to the Lord and fill your life with His unending peace, joy and wisdom to fulfil His divine purpose in life. May this book serve as a beacon of hope and light for all who read it, in Jesus Mighty Name. Amen!

CONTENTS

Dedication v
Acknowledgement xiii
Introduction xv

CHAPTER ONE
Nakedness *1*
    Nakedness as Original Purity 3
    Nakedness and the Fall of Humanity 5
    Nakedness as Openness to God 7
    Note these 8

CHAPTER TWO
Restoring the Significance of Nakedness *9*
    Reclaiming the Sacred Meaning of Nakedness in a Distorted Culture 10
    Reclaiming the Sacred Meaning of Nakedness:
    A Path to Redemption and Authenticity 12
    Note these 14

CHAPTER THREE
Understanding the Symbolism of Nakedness *15*
    Nakedness as Total Transparency 16
    Nakedness and the Absence of Shame 18
    Lessons for Modern Relationships 20
    Nakedness as a Spiritual Calling 21
    Note these 22

CHAPTER FOUR

Nakedness as a Symbol of Integrity and Simplicity 25

Nakedness as a Safeguard of Integrity 26

The Power of Transparency: Safeguarding Integrity
Through Vulnerability 28

Nakedness as a Reminder of Simplicity and Humility 29

Nakedness as a Call to Authenticity 31

Nakedness as a Message of Divine Purpose 33

Note these 35

CHAPTER FIVE

Nakedness as an Invitation to Approach God Openly 37

Nakedness as a Reminder of Life's Transience
and the Futility of Materialism 39

Nakedness and the Futility of Wealth 40

Nakedness as a Posture of Humility and Trust in
God's Sovereign Will 42

Nakedness and the Call to Eternal Perspective 44

CHAPTER SIX

Nakedness as the Ultimate Spiritual Lesson 47

Nakedness: Strips away Illusions of Self-sufficiency 49

Nakedness: Reminder of our needs for God's grace and presence 50

Nakedness as a Reflection of Our Beginning and End 52

Nakedness as an Acknowledgement of God's Sovereignty 53

Nakedness and Gratitude for Life's Blessings 55

Nakedness in Worship and Its Controversies 57

Nakedness as a Symbol of Purity and Sincerity 58

Note these 59

CHAPTER SEVEN
Nakedness and the Danger of Superficial Worship 61
Nakedness as Openness to God's Transformative Work 63
Nakedness and Worship in Spirit and Truth 64
True Nakedness in Worship: Sincerity, Humility, and Commitment 65
Worshiping in Truth: A Commitment to God's Will 66
Worshipping with a Pure Heart 68
Nakedness before God: Authentic Worship from the Heart 69
Note these 70

CHAPTER EIGHT
Nakedness as Openness and Surrender 73
Nakedness and the Transformation of the Heart 74
Nakedness as a Call to Align Faith and Action 76
Nakedness and Self-Reflection 77
Living in Spiritual Nakedness 78
Spiritual Transformation 79
Commitment to Integrity 81
Nakedness as a Symbol of Freedom from Societal Pressures 82
Nakedness as Vulnerability and Humility 84
Nakedness as a Call to Authentic Worship 85
Nakedness: A Return to Authenticity 86
Note these 87

CHAPTER NINE
Nakedness as Freedom in God's Truth 89
Complete Surrender: The Heart of True Devotion 90
Worshiping in Spirit and Truth: A Call for Genuine Devotion 92
Nakedness as Self-Examination: The Call to Authentic Faith 94

Nakedness: Vulnerability and Accountability in the Christian Faith 95
Note these 97

CHAPTER TEN
The Beauty of Spiritual Openness Before God 99

Embracing Vulnerability: The Power of
Openness in God's Presence 100
Nakedness as a Symbol of Renewal and Transformation 102
The Concept of Shedding the Old in Relationships 105
Nakedness as Contentment and Gratitude 106
Nakedness as Total Surrender and Openness in Relationships 108
Nakedness and the Effort Required for Transformation 110
Nakedness as a Thirst for God's Spirit 111
Note these 113

CHAPTER ELEVEN
Discernment in Relationships and Commitment 115

Living in Nakedness Before God and Others 117
Unity in Marriage: "Bone of My Bone and Flesh of My Flesh" 119
Adam's Commitment to Eve 120
The Wisdom of Unity 122
Note these 123

CHAPTER TWELVE
Healing in Relationships 125

Practical Wisdom Needed in Relationships 126
Prioritizing Love Over Material Things:
The Essence of True Relationships 131
Nakedness as the Ideal Relationship State 133
The Power of Human Connection and Spiritual Nakedness 134
Note these 136

CHAPTER THIRTEEN
God at the Center: The Key to Genuine Connection *137*
Spiritual Nakedness: Humility and Vulnerability 138
Christ's Love and the Symbolism of Nakedness in Marriage 140
Nakedness as Surrender: Letting God Lead 142
True Connection Through Spiritual Nakedness 143
Nakedness and the Intimate Relationship Christ Desires with Us 145
Note these 146

CHAPTER FOURTEEN
The Challenge of Spiritual Openness *147*
The Fleeting Nature of Spiritual Opportunity 150
Embracing Vulnerability: The Path to Purity and Transparency with God 152
Unity in God's Purpose: Embracing Spiritual Nakedness for True Connection 154
Spiritual Nakedness as the Key to Relationship and Life Success 155
Note these 157

Conclusion *159*

References *161*

Bible References *167*

Other Books by the Author *171*

Author's Profile *173*

ACKNOWLEDGEMENT

My deepest gratitude goes to God the Father, our Lord Jesus Christ, and the Holy Spirit, who have made me who I am today. Without His mercies and grace, I could not have come this far.

I am profoundly thankful to my wife, Rev. Mrs Yvonne Tweretwie, and our children, Cecilia Kyeretwie, Emmanuel Tweretwie, David Tweretwie, Samuel Tweretwie and Joseph Tweretwie for their unwavering love and tremendous support.

I extend heartfelt appreciation to Rev. Prof. Nana Kyei-Baffour, Healthcare Chaplain, Course Director of Postgraduate Education in Healthcare Chaplaincy, Adjunct Professor with Global University (Assemblies of God, USA), and Senior Pastor at Victory-City Assemblies of God, Wallington-London. He is an extraordinary mentor who consistently goes the extra mile to guide me in the right direction. May the Lord Almighty richly bless you for your invaluable presence in my life.

Not forgetting my Senior Pastor, Rev. Collins Okai, at Gospel Light Assemblies of God Church, Kumasi, Ghana, who nurtured me in my Christian life and walk with God.

Kudos to my spiritual children in the Lord, Vincent Eloh, Clifford Adom, Josephine Osei, Comfort Adusei and Juliet Adusei who are working tirelessly and immensely to advance this glorious assignment the Lord has given me.

Finally, I deeply cherish the love and support from the family of Miracle Temple Assemblies of God Church (MTAG), Milton Keynes, United Kingdom. Words cannot fully express my gratitude to them; their kindness and encouragement mean the world to me.

INTRODUCTION

Nakedness has been a subject of much debate and misconception across cultures and societies worldwide. Different individuals and communities have varied perceptions of what it truly means to be "naked," often associating it solely with physical exposure. But is that all there is to it? What if the concept of nakedness has a deeper, spiritual significance that transcends the surface? Throughout history, our understanding of nakedness has been clouded by misunderstanding, shame, and distorted views, but the Bible offers us a perspective that invites us to see nakedness in a new light, one that connects it to our relationship with God, others, and even ourselves. As we explore the essence of nakedness, we realize that it is more than just an outward state; it is a reflection of our inner vulnerability, transparency, and openness before the Creator.

In the Bible, the nakedness of Adam and Eve in the Garden of Eden holds deep spiritual meaning. When God created humanity, He made Adam and Eve naked, and *"the man and his wife were both naked, and they felt no shame"* (Genesis 2:25, NIV). This verse highlights the purity and intimacy of their original state free from shame, guilt, and fear. It is essential to understand that their nakedness was not just physical; it symbolized a deeper spiritual connection with God, untainted by sin. Unfortunately, when sin entered the world, Adam and Eve's nakedness was no longer an expression of purity, but of separation from God. The story of their fall demonstrates how the act of hiding their nakedness became a symbol of hiding from God and from each other. What does this tell us about the true nature of nakedness? Is it merely physical, or does it invite us to examine the state of our hearts before God?

As Christians, scholars, and individuals striving to live in alignment with God's will, there is a deep need to reclaim the true meaning of nakedness. It is not enough to view nakedness as something shameful or to associate it merely with the body. God calls us to embrace a deeper understanding, one that goes beyond the physical to touch on the spiritual aspects of our lives. In the pages of this book, *They Were Naked: The Language of Marital Unity*, we will explore the biblical and scholarly perspectives on nakedness, uncovering its significance in our lives, relationships, and marriages. Through a combination of biblical knowledge, scholarly insights, and philosophical reflections, we aim to unveil the transformative power of spiritual nakedness and how it can bring us closer to God, purify our hearts, and restore our relationships.

This book is divided into fourteen thought-provoking chapters, each shedding light on various aspects of nakedness. From "Nakedness as a Symbol of Integrity and Simplicity" to "Nakedness as the Ultimate Spiritual Lesson," these chapters will guide you through the multifaceted nature of nakedness in the context of faith and human connection. For instance, we explore how nakedness can be an invitation to approach God openly, shedding the masks of pride and self-sufficiency, and recognizing the beauty of spiritual openness. What does it mean to be spiritually naked before God? How can we embrace a life of purity, humility, and surrender in our relationships, especially in marriage? These questions will be explored in depth, offering insights that challenge our current perceptions and call us to a deeper, more authentic way of living.

I encourage you to read this book with an open heart, allowing the wisdom within these pages to transform your understanding of nakedness and its relevance in your life. As you reflect on the truths shared, may you be inspired to embrace spiritual nakedness, surrendering your pride, fears, and distractions to God. This book is not just for married couples or those in relationships, but for all of us who desire to walk in greater intimacy with God and live in purity, integrity, and transparency. God bless you as you embark on this journey of discovery and transformation.

CHAPTER ONE

NAKEDNESS

Nakedness is a deep concept that takes us back to the very beginning of humanity's story, which was created by God. While the word *"naked"* often carries an air of discomfort or misinterpretation today, it holds significant spiritual and symbolic meanings that shape our understanding of who we are in God's design. The concept of nakedness is first introduced in the Bible during the creation story. In the Garden of Eden, Adam and Eve were described as being naked and unashamed (Genesis 2:25, NIV): *"Adam and his wife were both naked, and they felt no shame."* This state of being reflects their innocence and the purity of their relationship with God and with each other. Their nakedness was a symbol of transparency, vulnerability, and the absence of sin. It represented humanity's original design, created to live in perfect harmony with God, untainted by guilt or fear. This view underscores that, in God's perfect creation, nakedness was not associated with shame but with freedom and openness in a divine relationship.

After Adam and Eve sinned by eating the forbidden fruit, their perception of nakedness changed dramatically. Genesis 3:7 states, *"Then the eyes of both of them were opened, and they realized they were naked; so they sewed fig leaves together and made coverings for themselves."* This shift marks the beginning of humanity's awareness of sin and separation from God. Nakedness now became a source of shame and vulnerability, symbolizing the brokenness of their relationship with their Creator. This perspective emphasizes that nakedness in a post-Fall world is often intertwined with guilt and a desire to hide from God, as seen when Adam and Eve hid themselves (Genesis 3:10, NIV): *"I heard you in the garden, and I was afraid because I was naked; so I hid."*

Moreover, throughout Scripture, nakedness is often used metaphorically to describe human vulnerability and exposure before God. In Ezekiel 16:8, NIV, God uses the imagery of clothing to describe His covenant with Israel: *"I spread the corner of my garment over you and covered your naked body. I gave you my solemn oath and entered into a covenant with you, declares the Sovereign Lord, and you became mine."* This passage highlights God's provision and grace, covering humanity's spiritual nakedness through His covenantal love. Similarly, Revelation 3:18 calls for believers to clothe themselves with righteousness: *"I counsel you to buy from me gold refined in the fire, so you can become rich; and white clothes to wear, so you can cover your shameful nakedness."* This underscores the need for divine intervention to restore humanity's dignity and purity. So, through Christ, the shame and guilt associated with nakedness are redeemed. Jesus bore the ultimate humiliation on the cross, where He was stripped of His garments, a symbol of taking on the shame of humanity (Matthew 27:28, NIV): *"They stripped him and put a scarlet robe on him."* His sacrifice restores believers to a state of righteousness, enabling them to stand unashamed before God. Romans 8:1 offers reassurance: *"Therefore, there is now no condemnation for those who are in Christ Jesus."* This redemption transforms nakedness into a reminder of God's grace, inviting believers to live in the freedom and confidence of their restored relationship with Him. The theme of nakedness, when viewed through the lens of redemption, emphasizes the journey from innocence, to shame, and back to divine covering through Christ's atonement. To fully explore this, let us break down the theme of nakedness into key points with examples, each offering deeper insight into its relevance.

NAKEDNESS AS ORIGINAL PURITY

In Genesis 2:25, *"Adam and his wife were both naked, and they felt no shame,"* reveals the profound state of purity and innocence in which humanity was created. This nakedness was not merely physical but symbolic of a transparent and unbroken relationship with God. Adam and Eve stood fully exposed before their Creator, not just in body but in soul and spirit, without fear, guilt, or the need to hide. It represented a life of perfect harmony free from the corruption of sin, shame, or deceit. This verse highlights the trust and vulnerability inherent in their relationship with God and with each other. They were completely open, reflecting the design of a life that relies fully on God's provision and love. Nakedness here is a symbol of purity, where nothing was concealed because there was no sin to obscure their integrity or disrupt their communion with God. It serves as a reminder of the original intent for humanity: to live in untainted fellowship with God, clothed only in His presence and grace.

Imagine a young child playing in a garden, their laughter ringing out as they explore freely, without any concern for judgment or fear. This image reflects the state of Adam and Eve in the Garden of Eden a life of innocence, untainted by sin, where they lived in perfect harmony with God and creation. Their nakedness was not just physical but symbolic of their transparency and purity. They had nothing to hide: no guilt to weigh them down, no shame to cover up, and no barriers to separate them from their Creator. In this state, they fully trusted God's provision and love, living in a relationship marked by openness and unity.

Their innocence mirrors that of a child who is unburdened by societal expectations or insecurities, simply enjoying the beauty and freedom of the moment. This purity highlights God's original design for humanity a relationship of complete trust and vulnerability, where His presence was the only covering, they needed. Nakedness in the Garden symbolized not only physical freedom but also the spiritual harmony that existed before the fall, a life where creation and Creator were intimately connected. Nakedness, as described in the story of creation, was not merely a physical state but a profound spiritual condition. It symbolized the transparency and openness with which Adam and Eve lived before God. They stood in His presence without shame, barriers, or fear, fully exposed yet fully accepted. This purity and vulnerability were reflections of their unbroken relationship with God, a bond unmarred by sin or guilt. In their nakedness, they embodied the trust and innocence that God intended for humanity a state of complete dependence on Him for identity, provision, and purpose.

This state of being also highlighted their perfect communion with God. They were free to walk and talk with Him, their lives intertwined with His divine presence. Nakedness represented a purity of spirit that required no concealment because there was nothing to hide. It was a declaration that their lives were fully aligned with God's will, a testimony to their faith and trust in His perfect plan. They were not just physically exposed; their hearts and souls were laid bare before their Creator, a reflection of the profound intimacy and honesty of their relationship.

The introduction of sin transformed the significance of nakedness from a state of innocence to one of guilt and shame. After Adam and Eve disobeyed God by eating the forbidden fruit, they immediately became aware of their nakedness and sought to cover themselves with fig leaves (Genesis 3:7, NIV): *"Then the eyes of both of them were opened, and they realized they were naked; so they sewed fig leaves together and made coverings for themselves."* This act symbolizes the onset of guilt and a desire to hide from God. Their nakedness, once a representation of purity and trust, became a painful reminder of their broken relationship with God. This shift illustrates the devastating effects of sin, which not only introduces shame but also erects barriers between humanity and their Creator, distorting the openness and transparency for which they were designed.

Despite the shame associated with sin, God's grace provides a path to restoration. In Genesis 3:21 (NIV), God demonstrates His mercy by clothing Adam and Eve with garments of skin: *"The Lord God made garments of skin for Adam and his wife and clothed them."* This act symbolizes God's provision and His desire to cover humanity's spiritual nakedness. In the New Testament, this restoration finds its ultimate expression in Christ, who offers believers a new covering through His sacrifice. Romans 13:14 (NIV) encourages us to *"clothe yourselves with the Lord Jesus Christ."* Through Jesus, we are restored to a state of righteousness, enabling us to stand before God without fear or shame. Nakedness, when viewed through this lens, becomes a reminder of God's redemptive power and His longing for us to live in intimacy, purity, and trust with Him.

NAKEDNESS AND THE FALL OF HUMANITY

When Adam and Eve sinned by eating the forbidden fruit, their first instinct was to cover their nakedness (Genesis 3:7, NIV): *"Then the eyes of both of them were opened, and they realized they were naked; so they sewed fig leaves together and made coverings for themselves."* This response signifies more than a physical act; it marks humanity's loss of innocence and the birth of shame. Before the fall, Adam and Eve were described as naked but unashamed (Genesis 2:25, NIV): *"Adam and his wife were both naked, and they felt no shame."* Why did this innocence vanish so abruptly? Their disobedience not only altered their relationship with God but also distorted their view of themselves. Suddenly, what had been pure and natural became a source of discomfort, fear, and insecurity. The question arises: How often do we, like Adam and Eve, try to cover our vulnerabilities instead of turning to God for healing and restoration?

The shift from unashamed openness to self-conscious hiding also reflects the broader consequences of sin alienation. The fig leaves Adam and Eve used to cover themselves symbolize humanity's attempts to solve spiritual problems with inadequate, self-made solutions. Why did they hide from the very God who created them? Genesis 3:10 (NIV) records

Adam's response to God's presence: *"I heard you in the garden, and I was afraid because I was naked; so I hid."* This fear and separation highlight the chasm sin creates between humanity and God. Yet, even in their fallen state, God initiated restoration by providing garments of skin to clothe them (Genesis 3:21, NIV): *"The Lord God made garments of skin for Adam and his wife and clothed them."* Does this not show a God who is both just and merciful, offering grace even when humanity chooses rebellion? This narrative urges us to reflect on whether we are hiding from God or trusting Him to cover our vulnerabilities and restore our relationship with Him.

Consider a situation where someone has done something wrong and instinctively tries to cover it up whether by hiding evidence, making excuses, or avoiding confrontation. This behavior mirrors Adam and Eve's response to their sin. Just as they used fig leaves to conceal their nakedness and hid from God in the garden (Genesis 3:8), people often resort to similar tactics to escape accountability. For instance, a child who breaks a vase might hide the pieces and feign ignorance when questioned. These actions reflect the universal human tendency to avoid exposure and judgment. The desire to conceal wrongdoing stems from an internal acknowledgement of guilt and a fear of consequences.

The covering of their nakedness was symbolic of humanity's fractured relationship with God. Sin introduced guilt and alienation, altering how humans relate to their Creator and to one another. The fig leaves Adam and Eve used were inadequate coverings, signifying humanity's inability to address sin on its own. This action highlights the instinctive drive to protect oneself from perceived judgment, yet it also underscores the futility of self-reliance in restoring broken relationships. Today, this tendency manifests in various ways such as projecting an idealized image, avoiding vulnerability, or rejecting help. These behaviors create barriers in relationships, distancing us from others and from God. Reflecting on this narrative invites us to confront our own defenses and strive for genuine reconciliation, embracing God's grace and seeking transparency with others.

NAKEDNESS AS OPENNESS TO GOD

Nakedness is also a metaphor for complete honesty and vulnerability before God. This concept is vividly illustrated in Psalm 139:23-24, where David prays, *"Search me, God, and know my heart; test me and know my anxious thoughts."* Here, nakedness symbolizes spiritual transparency—laying bare one's innermost thoughts, struggles, and desires before the Creator. Unlike physical nakedness, which may evoke discomfort or shame, spiritual nakedness is an act of trust and surrender. It acknowledges that God already knows everything about us (Psalm 139:1-4) and invites Him into our lives to reveal what needs healing or correction. This vulnerability is not about weakness but about allowing God to work in our lives without barriers.

Imagine two close friends who share their deepest fears and aspirations without fear of judgment. How do such relationships flourish? Trust and mutual respect create an atmosphere of safety, allowing authenticity to thrive. In the same way, our relationship with God grows deeper when we approach Him with honesty and humility. Yet, how often do we, like Adam and Eve, try to hide our struggles from God? The Bible assures us in 1 John 1:9 (NIV): *"If we confess our sins, He is faithful and just and will forgive us our sins and purify us from all unrighteousness."* Confession is not about exposing ourselves to condemnation but about stepping into God's grace and allowing His transformative power to work in our lives. When we let go of our fears and open our hearts to Him, we experience the depth of His forgiveness and a renewed intimacy with Him.

Spiritual nakedness is an invitation to lay down the masks we wear and dismantle the walls we build to shield ourselves from perceived rejection. But isn't it freeing to know that God's acceptance of us is unwavering? As Romans 8:1 (NIV) declares, *"Therefore, there is now no condemnation for those who are in Christ Jesus."* When we trust in this truth, we are empowered to be vulnerable before Him, knowing His love is unconditional. This kind of transparency requires courage; it asks us to relinquish control and place our dependence on God. But through this surrender, we discover true freedom, freedom to live as fully known and fully loved children of God. Isn't this the kind of authentic relationship our souls truly long for? By embracing spiritual nakedness, we find the strength to be who God created us to be, unencumbered by fear or shame.

Spiritual nakedness, in practical terms, is about approaching God with complete honesty in prayer and worship, shedding all pretense and masks. It involves sharing our joys, fears, failures, and hopes openly, trusting in His boundless mercy and grace. The Bible reassures us of this in Hebrews 4:16 (NIV): *"Let us then approach God's throne of grace with confidence, so that we may receive mercy and find grace to help us in our time of need."* By confessing our sins and vulnerabilities, we acknowledge that God's mercy far surpasses our guilt, leading to healing and restoration. This openness with God not only strengthens our spiritual connection but also transforms our relationships with others. It empowers us to engage authentically, mirroring the transparency and grace we receive from God. As we align ourselves with His will through this practice, we become more attuned to His purpose, reflecting His love and compassion in our daily lives.

NOTE THESE

Innocence and Purity – Humanity was originally created in a state of purity and openness, without guilt or shame.

Trust in God – Nakedness symbolized complete reliance on God's provision, presence, and love.

The Impact of Sin – Sin introduced shame, fear, and separation, altering humanity's relationship with God.

God's Grace and Redemption – Despite sin, God provides a covering, ultimately fulfilled through Christ's sacrifice.

Spiritual Transparency – True intimacy with God requires honesty, surrender, and openness in our relationship with Him.

CHAPTER TWO

RESTORING THE SIGNIFICANCE OF NAKEDNESS

In today's world, nakedness has been stripped of its original meaning and often reduced to something scandalous or inappropriate. This shift reflects a cultural departure from the biblical perspective of nakedness as a symbol of purity, vulnerability, and intimacy with God. In the Garden of Eden, Adam and Eve's nakedness represented their innocence and unbroken communion with their Creator (Genesis 2:25). However, sin distorted this ideal, introducing shame and the desire to cover oneself. Over time, society has further distorted the concept of nakedness, associating it predominantly with shame, exploitation, or objectification. This reduction reveals how deeply humanity's understanding of God's original design has been marred by sin. It is a stark reminder of the spiritual and moral consequences of straying from God's intentions.

Restoring the significance of nakedness invites us to reflect on God's original design for humanity a state of innocence and unbroken communion with Him. In the Garden of Eden, nakedness symbolized purity and vulnerability, representing a relationship free from fear and shame (Genesis 2:25, NIV): *"Adam and his wife were both naked, and they felt no shame."* But how often do we, in our modern lives, view vulnerability as a weakness rather than the foundation of genuine relationships? The shift from purity to shame caused by sin serves as a poignant reminder of humanity's departure from God's intentions. It challenges us to reclaim the biblical view of nakedness not merely as physical exposure, but as spiritual transparency and openness before God. Are we willing to lay aside the figurative "fig leaves" we use to hide from Him and others?

For current and future generations, this understanding offers crucial lessons about identity, modesty, and trust. How can we restore a godly perspective in a world that often prioritizes superficial appearances over the heart's posture? Romans 12:2 (NIV) reminds us: *"Do not conform to the pattern of this world, but be transformed by the renewing of your mind."* This transformation calls us to align our thoughts with God's truth, seeing nakedness as a metaphor for living in authenticity and dependence on Him. Teaching future generations this perspective will help them resist the cultural pressures that distort the value of the human body and relationships. By understanding and embracing God's design, we create a legacy of spiritual integrity, reminding others that true worth comes from God's view of us not the world's distorted lens.

RECLAIMING THE SACRED MEANING OF NAKEDNESS IN A DISTORTED CULTURE

In today's world, the concept of nakedness has been stripped of its sacred and symbolic value, often reduced to a tool for exploitation or sensationalism. Media and cultural narratives have transformed nakedness into a representation of vulnerability that is frequently exploited for profit or sensational purposes, detaching it from its biblical origins. However, Scripture reminds us that nakedness originally symbolized purity, openness, and intimacy with God. Genesis 2:25 (NIV) states, *"Adam and his wife were both naked, and they felt no shame,"* reflecting a state of perfect trust and communion with their Creator. To reclaim this sacred meaning, Christians are called to reject cultural distortions and instead focus on the deeper spiritual truths associated with transparency and authenticity before God. This involves acknowledging that the shame introduced by sin has been replaced by the grace and righteousness offered through Christ (2 Corinthians 5:21, NIV): *"God made him who had no sin to be sin for us so that in him we might become the righteousness of God."*

Famous Christian authors also highlight the importance of living transparently before God and resisting the pressures of worldly conformity. A.W. Tozer wrote, *"We must hide nothing from God and, even more important, we must see to it that we hide nothing from ourselves."* This quote underscores the necessity of spiritual nakedness an unreserved openness before God, where His transformative power can work fully in our lives. By reclaiming this perspective, Christians are better equipped to model modesty, respect, and authenticity, offering a counter-narrative to the distorted cultural views of nakedness. Ultimately, this reclamation points to the hope of eternal restoration, as Revelation 21:3-4 (NIV) assures us of a time when God will dwell with humanity, eradicating all shame, sin, and separation: "He will wipe every tear from their eyes. There will be no more death or mourning or crying or pain, for the old order of things has passed away."

As Christians, we are called to reclaim the deeper meaning of nakedness, viewing it not through a lens of cultural distortion but as a reminder of our spiritual journey. Restoring the significance of nakedness begins with understanding its biblical context. Nakedness, in its original state, symbolized a complete openness to God and each other a state of being fully known and fully accepted. For believers, this serves as a powerful metaphor for spiritual restoration. Through Christ, the shame introduced by sin is replaced with grace and forgiveness. The call to reclaim nakedness is, therefore, not about physical exposure but about rediscovering the spiritual posture of vulnerability and honesty before God.

This reclamation challenges Christians to reflect on their relationship with God. Are there areas in their lives where they still feel the need to hide or cover up? Nakedness in this sense is a reminder to strip away pretense, pride, and fear, allowing God to work in and through their weaknesses. It invites believers to embrace their identity in Christ, who offers them righteousness in place of their inadequacies (2 Corinthians 5:21).

RECLAIMING THE SACRED MEANING OF NAKEDNESS: A PATH TO REDEMPTION AND AUTHENTICITY

Restoring the significance of nakedness begins with rejecting cultural distortions and embracing biblical truth about human worth and identity. Today, societal perceptions often reduce nakedness to physical exposure, associating it with shame or objectification. How did we move so far from God's original design? Genesis 1:27 (NIV) reminds us, *"So God created mankind in his own image, in the image of God he created them; male and female he created them."* This verse underscores that our worth lies in being God's creation, not in worldly perceptions. Christians have a responsibility to teach the next generation this truth, fostering environments where people are valued for who they are rather than how they appear. In such spaces, respect, modesty, and authenticity take center stage, providing a safe haven where individuals can live without fear of judgment or exploitation.

Reclaiming the spiritual meaning of nakedness also offers hope for restoration through Christ. In the beginning, Adam and Eve's nakedness symbolized purity and uninhibited communion with God. Sin shattered that, introducing shame and separation. But through Christ's sacrifice, this separation is bridged, and the promise of eternal restoration is offered. Revelation 21:3-4 (NIV) describes this ultimate hope: *"And I heard a loud voice from the throne saying, 'Look! God's dwelling place is now among the people, and he will dwell with them. They will be his people, and God himself will be with them and be their God. He will wipe every tear from their eyes."* This vision reminds believers that nakedness, in its spiritual sense, is not a source of shame but a sign of complete redemption and acceptance in God's presence.

What does this mean for Christians living today? It calls them to reflect God's love and redemption by living transparently and authentically before Him and others. Are there areas where we still hide, fearful of rejection? As we embrace the truth of our identity in Christ, we are challenged to shed pride, pretense, and fear, reflecting the beauty of God's grace. Living with spiritual transparency also equips believers to be witnesses to a broken world, modeling what it means to be fully known and fully loved by God. In doing so, Christians not only reclaim the sacred meaning of nakedness but also inspire others to walk in the freedom and dignity that comes from knowing their Creator.

Living transparently and authentically as Christians begins with embracing the truth of our identity in Christ. When we understand that we are fearfully and wonderfully made (Psalm 139:14, NIV), we can shed the masks of insecurity and pride that often hinder us from fully engaging with God and others. This act of vulnerability aligns with the call in 2 Corinthians 5:17 (NIV), which reminds us, *"Therefore, if anyone is in Christ, the new creation has come: The old has gone, the new is here!"* Living as a new creation means discarding the remnants of sin's shame and walking boldly in the light of God's love, free from fear of rejection or judgment.

Furthermore, this transparency is not just a personal endeavor; it has profound implications for our relationships. When Christians model spiritual authenticity, they create environments where others feel safe to share their struggles and victories. James 5:16 (NIV) encourages believers to *"confess your sins to each other and pray for each other so that you may be healed."* This mutual openness fosters a culture of grace, where God's love and redemption are evident in the lives of His people. In a world that often celebrates pretense and perfection, the church is called to be a beacon of authenticity, demonstrating that true freedom comes from living in alignment with God's truth.

Therefore, living authentically before God equips believers to be effective witnesses to a broken and searching world. As Matthew 5:14-16 (NIV) declares, *"You are the light of the world. A town built on a hill cannot be hidden. Neither do people light a lamp and put it under a bowl. Instead, they put it on its stand, and it gives light to everyone in the house. In the same way, let your light shine before others, that they may see your good deeds and glorify your Father in heaven."* By reflecting God's grace through their transparency, Christians point others to the transformative power of the gospel. This lifestyle not only reclaims the sacred meaning of spiritual nakedness but also inspires others to embrace their identity in Christ, fostering a community grounded in love, respect, and dignity.

NOTE THESE

Our worth comes from God – Human value is based on being created in God's image, not on worldly standards.

Christ restores what sin broke – Through Jesus, believers can overcome shame and embrace spiritual transparency.

Authenticity deepens relationships – Living truthfully before God and others fosters trust and healing.

The church should model grace – A culture of honesty and acceptance encourages spiritual growth and restoration.

Faith shines through transparency – Living openly in Christ reflects His light to a world in need of redemption.

CHAPTER THREE

Understanding the Symbolism of Nakedness

Nakedness, as described in the biblical account of Adam and Eve, is deeply symbolic. It transcends the physical state and delves into the realms of purity, openness, and trust. In Genesis 2:25, it states, "And they were both naked, the man and his wife, and were not ashamed." This verse provides a framework for understanding God's intentional design for humanity and relationships. Nakedness in the biblical context symbolizes a state of innocence and unbroken fellowship with God. Before the fall, Adam and Eve's nakedness reflected their pure relationship with their Creator and each other. They had nothing to hide because there was no sin, shame, or guilt. Genesis 2:25 (NLT) states, *"Now the man and his wife were both naked, but they felt no shame."* This verse highlights that nakedness represented vulnerability without fear, a profound trust in God's provision, and an authentic connection with each other. It was a state of perfect transparency, showing humanity as God intended completely open and dependent on Him. This symbolism serves as a reminder of the harmony we were created to enjoy with God and others before sin disrupted that balance.

However, after sin entered the world, nakedness took on a new meaning. It became associated with shame and the desire to hide, as seen in Genesis 3:7 (NLT): *"At that moment their eyes were opened, and they suddenly felt shame at their nakedness. So they sewed fig leaves together to cover themselves."* This shift reflects how sin distorts God's original design, replacing purity and trust with guilt and fear. For Christians today, understanding the symbolism of nakedness challenges us to reflect on our spiritual state. Are we striving to return to a posture of openness with God, or are we hiding behind the "fig leaves" of pride, fear, or self-sufficiency? Recognizing the deeper meaning of nakedness encourages us to embrace transparency with God and others, allowing His grace to restore the harmony lost through sin.

NAKEDNESS AS TOTAL TRANSPARENCY

Nakedness symbolizes complete transparency in relationships, reflecting the openness and vulnerability God desires in human connections. In Genesis 2:23, when Adam first saw Eve, his declaration *"This is now bone of my bones and flesh of my flesh"* captures the depth of their connection. This recognition was instinctive and unguarded, highlighting the absence of barriers between them. Their nakedness was not merely physical but also relational, representing their ability to fully see, know, and accept one another without fear or shame. This transparency exemplifies the ideal of relationships as God intended: rooted in truth, trust, and mutual respect. Nakedness in this context is a metaphor for the freedom to be fully known and still completely loved, a state of harmony that mirrors the intimacy God seeks with His creation.

In a relationship where there are no secrets or hidden agendas, trust becomes the cornerstone. The absence of emotional walls fosters genuine intimacy, as both individuals feel safe to be their authentic selves. This transparency mirrors the state of Adam and Eve before the fall, described in Genesis 2:25 (NLT): *"Now the man and his wife were both naked, but they felt no shame."* Their vulnerability with one another reflected a relationship built on mutual acceptance and trust, untainted by sin or fear. When one partner shares their fears or insecurities, and the other responds with empathy and understanding, the relationship deepens. This openness creates an atmosphere where love and respect flourish, forming a bond that can withstand challenges.

Transparency also eliminates the barriers of pretense and misunderstanding that often plague relationships. Secrets and hidden motives can erode trust, creating distance between partners. Proverbs 27:5 (NLT) reminds us, *"An open rebuke is better than hidden love."* This verse highlights the importance of honesty in maintaining a healthy relationship, even when it involves confronting uncomfortable truths. True intimacy is not about presenting a perfect facade but about offering one's true self, knowing they are valued and accepted despite their imperfections. Such openness requires vulnerability, but it also builds resilience, as both individuals learn to navigate challenges together with grace and humility.

For Christians, this type of transparency is not only a model for human relationships but also reflects the relationship God desires with His people. Hebrews 4:13 (NLT) states, *"Nothing in all creation is hidden from God. Everything is naked and exposed before His eyes, and He is the one to whom we are accountable."* Just as God sees and loves us in our entirety, so should we strive to create relationships that prioritize honesty, grace, and understanding. By embracing this principle, couples and individuals alike can build stronger connections that honor God and reflect His love.

Nakedness in the garden illustrates that relationships thrive on truthfulness and vulnerability. The transparency between Adam and Eve before the fall reveals a profound truth: authentic relationships require openness. When sin entered the picture, this transparency was shattered, replaced by shame, blame, and hiding (Genesis 3:7-12). The resulting barriers reflect the struggles many relationships face today miscommunication, mistrust, and emotional distance. Yet, the example of nakedness in Eden invites us to strive for restoration by prioritizing vulnerability and truth in our connections.

For Christians, this principle is especially relevant in marriage, where the relationship is meant to reflect the union between Christ and His

Church (Ephesians 5:25-27). Nakedness as total transparency encourages couples to pursue a relationship marked by honesty, humility, and sacrificial love. It also extends beyond marriage, offering a model for friendships, family connections, and community life. When people interact with openness and authenticity, they reflect God's design for relationships and create spaces where love and trust can flourish.

Ultimately, the symbolism of nakedness calls individuals to evaluate the state of their relationships. Are there areas where fear, pride, or past hurts have built walls? By embracing the transparency demonstrated in Eden, believers can work toward relationships that are not only truthful but also transformative. Through God's grace, these relationships can mirror the harmony and intimacy He intended from the beginning, serving as a testament to His love and faithfulness.

NAKEDNESS AND THE ABSENCE OF SHAME

One of the most striking aspects of Adam and Eve's state before the fall was their lack of shame, highlighting a condition of dignity and mutual respect. In Genesis 2:25, the Bible describes Adam and Eve as being "naked and unashamed." This lack of shame is significant because it indicates a state of complete harmony both with each other and with God. Their nakedness symbolized not only physical openness but also spiritual and emotional transparency. There was no fear of judgment, rejection, or comparison, as their identity and worth were grounded in their perfect relationship with God. This state reflects God's original design for humanity: a life free from the distortions of sin, where dignity and mutual respect are foundational to relationships.

Before the fall, Adam and Eve experienced a profound freedom in their nakedness, marked by the absence of shame. In Genesis 2:25 (NLT), it says, *"Now the man and his wife were both naked, but they felt no shame."* This statement carries deep spiritual and emotional significance, illustrating that their relationship with one another and with God was unhindered by the fear of judgment or the burden of insecurity. Their nakedness was not just physical but symbolic of complete vulnerability, where they were fully known and accepted by each other and their Creator. It is hard to imagine a world where shame does not cloud human interactions, isn't it? Without shame, Adam and Eve were able to live in pure, untainted communion, reflecting God's original intention for humanity's relationships grounded in love, respect, and freedom.

The absence of shame in Adam and Eve's relationship is a direct reflection of the dignity and respect that God desires in human relationships. This idea of transparent, shame-free connection is what God originally intended for all His creations. However, sin introduced shame, hiding, and fear, distorting the original design. But can we reclaim this kind of open, shame-free relationship with one another and with God today? 1 John 1:9 (NLT) offers hope, saying, *"But if we confess our sins to Him, He is faithful and just to forgive us our sins and to cleanse us from all wickedness."* Through Christ, we are offered a path back to that unashamed state where we can approach God and others with honesty, knowing we are covered by His grace. This understanding can transform how we view ourselves and our relationships, allowing us to live without the weight of shame and to honor the dignity with which we were created.

So, shame only entered the picture after Adam and Eve disobeyed God (Genesis 3:7). This sudden awareness of their nakedness and their instinct to cover themselves revealed how sin fractured their sense of identity and their relationship with God. Shame became a barrier, not just between them and God, but also between one another. What was once a condition of mutual respect and vulnerability was replaced by fear, insecurity, and the need to hide. This transformation underscores the profound impact of sin on human relationships and self-perception.

Think of a child who feels no embarrassment in their natural state. Children often exhibit a beautiful innocence, moving through life unburdened by self-consciousness or guilt. They have no concept of shame because their sense of identity has not yet been shaped by societal judgments or personal failures. This innocence mirrors the pre-fall state of Adam and Eve. Just as a child trusts their caregivers and finds security in their unconditional love, Adam and Eve found their sense of worth and dignity in their Creator. Their lack of shame was not naivety but a reflection of their perfect communion with God. This analogy reminds us of the freedom and joy that comes from living without the weight of shame.

Adam and Eve's unashamed nakedness reflects the unbroken communion they shared with God and each other, teaching us the importance of embracing who we are in God's eyes. Shame often distorts our perception of ourselves and others, leading to insecurity, fear, and isolation. In contrast, the absence of shame allows us to live in the freedom of knowing that our worth is not determined by external factors but by our identity as God's creation. When we embrace who we are in God's eyes, we can reject the false standards imposed by society and overcome self-doubt. This mindset enables us to build relationships based on authenticity and mutual respect, mirroring the harmony of Eden.

For Christians, the redemption offered through Christ restores the possibility of living without shame. By confessing our sins and accepting God's grace, we are freed from the guilt and self-consciousness that sin brings (Romans 8:1). This freedom enables us to approach God and others with confidence, knowing that we are fully known and fully loved. It also challenges us to extend the same grace and acceptance to others, fostering relationships marked by dignity and respect.

LESSONS FOR MODERN RELATIONSHIPS

The principles of purity, transparency, and freedom from shame in Adam and Eve's narrative remain profoundly relevant for modern relationships. In a world often marked by superficial connections, miscommunication, and hidden agendas, these principles provide a timeless framework for building strong and meaningful bonds. Purity in relationships encourages motives rooted in love and respect, free from selfishness or manipulation. Transparency fosters an atmosphere of honesty and vulnerability, while freedom from shame creates a foundation where individuals feel valued and accepted for who they are. These elements work together to cultivate trust, an essential component of any healthy relationship.

Imagine a couple who practices complete honesty in their communication. They openly share their thoughts, feelings, and struggles without fear of judgment or rejection. This level of openness creates a safe space where both partners feel understood and supported. For instance, if one partner admits a mistake or expresses concern, the other responds with compassion and a willingness to work through the issue together. This dynamic mirrors the relational nakedness Adam and Eve experienced before the fall, where their transparency reflected mutual respect and trust. Such honesty strengthens the bond between individuals, helping them navigate challenges with unity and grace.

The relational nakedness of Adam and Eve underscores the importance of truthfulness in nurturing healthy bonds. Their openness before sin illustrates an ideal of intimacy untainted by fear or distrust. Modern relationships often falter when dishonesty, secrecy, or unresolved shame creeps in, creating barriers to genuine connection. By embracing the principles exemplified in Eden, individuals can work toward relationships characterized by authenticity and mutual understanding.

Transparency encourages accountability and reduces misunderstandings, while freedom from shame allows people to share their true selves without fear of rejection. Purity in intentions ensures that interactions are guided by love and a desire for the other's well-being. These principles challenge us to examine our motives, practice humility, and prioritize communication in our relationships.

NAKEDNESS AS A SPIRITUAL CALLING

Nakedness is a relational concept but a profound spiritual calling, inviting us to stand before God as we truly are transparent, humble, and unafraid. The state of Adam and Eve's unashamed nakedness in the garden reflects the ideal relationship God desires with humanity:

one of complete openness and trust. Their innocence before the fall allowed them to approach God without fear or pretense, embodying the purity of a heart fully aligned with its Creator. Similarly, we are called to present ourselves honestly before God, acknowledging our flaws, weaknesses, and sins, knowing that His love and grace cover all. This spiritual nakedness requires humility a willingness to set aside pride and self-reliance, and the courage to confront our vulnerabilities in His presence.

Nakedness challenges us to live lives marked by purity, transparency, and the absence of shame. Spiritually, this means approaching God without masks or defenses, trusting in His unconditional love. It also means rejecting the shame and fear that sin often instills. Through Christ, we are offered redemption and the freedom to stand confidently before God, no longer defined by our past or our failings (Hebrews 4:16).

In our relationships, embracing the concept of nakedness involves fostering genuine connections based on truth and humility. When we live authentically both with God and others we reflect His original design for humanity, marked by dignity and unbroken communion. This understanding transforms how we view vulnerability, shifting it from a source of fear to an avenue for deeper intimacy with God and those around us.

Ultimately, rediscovering the spiritual significance of nakedness reminds us of the beauty of living as God intended: free, open, and unashamed in His presence. It is an invitation to embrace our true selves and to trust in the transformative power of His love and grace.

NOTE THESE

Honesty builds trust – Transparency in relationships fosters open communication and deepens trust between individuals.

Purity strengthens love – Genuine motives based on love and respect prevent manipulation and selfishness in relationships.

Freedom from shame fosters connection – Being open and vulnerable without fear allows for stronger emotional and spiritual bonds.

Authenticity nurtures intimacy – Living truthfully before God and others leads to deeper, more meaningful connections.

God's grace removes fear – Standing before God in humility and trust enables us to live free from guilt and shame.

CHAPTER FOUR

NAKEDNESS AS A SYMBOL OF INTEGRITY AND SIMPLICITY

Nakedness, as depicted in the Bible, symbolizes a heart laid bare, unencumbered by deceit or pretense. In Genesis 2:25 (NLT), it is written, *"Now the man and his wife were both naked, but they felt no shame."* This state of nakedness was an emblem of their integrity and simplicity living in total alignment with God's will, free from the complexities and corruptions introduced by sin. Integrity, in this sense, means being the same inside and out, reflecting honesty and consistency in all areas of life. Transparency is not just a human virtue; it is foundational to a relationship with God. The psalmist echoes this sentiment, saying, *"Create in me a clean heart, O God. Renew a loyal spirit within me" (Psalm 51:10, NLT).* Nakedness, therefore, invites us to live authentically, unhindered by fear or falsehood, both before God and others.

Simplicity is another vital aspect symbolized by nakedness. It reflects a life unburdened by unnecessary distractions or material attachments, which can obscure our relationship with God. In a world overwhelmed by materialism and superficiality, the imagery of nakedness calls us back to a state of purity and purpose. Oswald Chambers, a renowned Christian author, once wrote, *"Simplicity is the secret to seeing things clearly."* Stripping away the layers of complication in our lives allows us to focus on what truly matters our walk with God and our service to others. Jesus Himself emphasized this principle when He said, *"Seek the Kingdom of God above all else, and live righteously, and He will give you everything you need" (Matthew 6:33, NLT).* Nakedness, in its symbolic sense, becomes a powerful reminder to prioritize God and live with singular devotion.

Moreover, nakedness underscores humility, an essential posture for approaching God. To stand spiritually naked before God requires an acknowledgement of our dependence on Him and a surrender of pride and self-sufficiency. Andrew Murray, in his book *Humility: The Beauty of Holiness*, writes, *"Humility is the only soil in which grace takes root; the lack of humility is the sufficient explanation of every defect and failure."* Nakedness as humility frees us from the need to exalt ourselves, allowing God's grace to shine through our lives. The apostle Paul reinforces this truth in 2 Corinthians 12:9 (NLT): *"Each time He said, 'My grace is all you need. My power works best in weakness.' So now I am glad to boast about my weaknesses, so that the power of Christ can work through me."* Nakedness as a symbol of integrity, simplicity, and humility challenges us to live a life fully surrendered to God, embracing His grace and reflecting His glory.

NAKEDNESS AS A SAFEGUARD OF INTEGRITY

Nakedness as a symbol of transparency emphasizes the importance of integrity in all areas of life, fostering trust and accountability. In a workplace context, specialized clothing such as uniforms or protective gear symbolizes clarity, accountability, and adherence to established standards. These measures ensure transparency by eliminating doubt and ambiguity about roles and responsibilities. Spiritually, nakedness reflects a similar idea: living a life where actions and intentions are open to scrutiny, aligning with God's standards. Proverbs 10:9 (NLT) states, *"People with integrity walk safely, but those who follow crooked paths will be exposed."* Just as cleanrooms demand meticulous practices to maintain purity, so too does integrity requires a commitment to honesty and alignment with God's principles.

In relationships, especially within marriage, nakedness is a profound symbol of openness and trust. The transparency represented by nakedness allows couples to be fully known and fully loved, fostering an environment where vulnerability is not feared but embraced. Genesis 2:25 (NLT) says, *"Now the man and his wife were both naked, but they felt no shame."* This verse captures the purity and trust that characterized the first human relationship before sin entered the world. When spouses commit to openness and honesty, they reflect this original design, creating a strong foundation for intimacy and unity. As Christian author Gary Chapman states in *The Five Love Languages*, *"When we choose to be transparent, we create an opportunity for intimacy to grow."*

The concept of nakedness as a safeguard of integrity also applies to the broader Christian life. Living transparently before God and others ensures that we remain accountable, fostering a life of integrity that reflects God's character. Hebrews 4:13 (NLT) reminds us, *"Nothing in all creation is hidden from God. Everything is naked and exposed before His eyes, and He is the one to whom we are accountable."* This verse underscores the importance of living with integrity, knowing that God sees and values truthfulness in all we do. Renowned theologian A.W. Tozer once wrote, *"Integrity is the foundation of character; it is doing the right thing when no one is watching."* By embracing transparency, believers not only honor God but also model authenticity to others, inspiring trust and respect.

So, nakedness as a safeguard of integrity challenges we as Christians to examine their own lives for areas of secrecy or pretense. Are there aspects of our character or relationships where we avoid transparency due to fear of judgment or rejection? Embracing spiritual nakedness before God enables us to shed these barriers and grow in grace. Jesus said in Matthew 5:8 (NLT), *"God blesses those whose hearts are pure, for they will see God."* Purity of heart, rooted in transparency and integrity, positions us to experience God's presence and blessings more fully. By living openly and authentically, we not only safeguard our own integrity but also encourage others to pursue lives marked by honesty, humility, and grace.

THE POWER OF TRANSPARENCY: SAFEGUARDING INTEGRITY THROUGH VULNERABILITY

When two individuals commit to being fully open with one another, they establish a foundation of trust that mirrors God's design for authentic relationships. Transparency enables both parties to feel valued and secure, knowing they can share their thoughts, struggles, and vulnerabilities without fear of rejection. This dynamic was evident in the friendship between David and Jonathan. In 1 Samuel 18:3-4 (NLT), we read, *"And Jonathan made a solemn pact with David, because he loved him as he loved himself. Jonathan sealed the pact by taking off his robe and giving it to David, together with his tunic, sword, bow, and belt."* Jonathan's gesture symbolized his transparency and commitment to the relationship, placing David's well-being above his own. How might our relationships change if we approached them with this level of openness and selflessness? As Christian author Dietrich Bonhoeffer once wrote, *"The person who loves their dream of community will destroy community, but the person who loves those around them will create community."*

Nakedness as a safeguard of integrity transcends physical openness and speaks to the heart of humility and authenticity. Consider the story of Peter after his denial of Jesus. When Jesus resurrected, Peter could have hidden in shame, but he chose to meet Jesus on the shores of Galilee (John 21:15-19, NLT). There, Jesus restored Peter by asking him three times, "Do you love me?" This moment highlights the power of vulnerability and humility in restoring integrity and trust. Peter's willingness to confront his failure and accept Jesus' grace allowed him to step into his calling with renewed confidence. How often do we resist vulnerability out of fear of judgment, not realizing it is the very thing that leads to healing and growth?

In marriage, this principle is especially vital. Nakedness as a safeguard of integrity fosters deeper intimacy, as seen in the relationship between Ruth and Boaz. Ruth's openness about her situation and her trust in Boaz's character laid the groundwork for their bond (Ruth 3:9-11, NLT). Boaz's response, recognizing Ruth's integrity and showing respect for her, exemplifies the mutual accountability that strengthens relationships. This level of transparency invites God's blessings into the relationship, aligning it with His original intent for marriage. As Christian author Gary Thomas writes in *Sacred Marriage*, *"What if God designed marriage to make us holy more than to make us happy?"* Transparency helps couples grow spiritually as they align their relationship with God's purpose.

Therefore, nakedness as a safeguard of integrity calls us to examine our personal relationships with God. Are we transparent with Him about our struggles, doubts, and fears? Adam and Eve's story reminds us of the consequences of hiding from God. In Genesis 3:9-10 (NLT), when God asked, *"Where are you?"* Adam admitted, "I hid because I was naked." Unlike Adam, David embraced transparency with God, as reflected in Psalm 139:23-24 (NLT*): "Search me, O God, and know my heart; test me and know my anxious thoughts. Point out anything in me that offends you, and lead me along the path of everlasting life."* When we come to God with honesty and humility, we safeguard our spiritual integrity, opening ourselves to His transformative grace. This level of transparency inspires us to live authentically before others, modeling a life rooted in God's truth and love.

NAKEDNESS AS A REMINDER OF SIMPLICITY AND HUMILITY

Nakedness profoundly symbolizes the essence of simplicity and humility. From birth, humans arrive in the world with nothing, a state that reflects their inherent dependency and vulnerability. This natural condition reminds us of life's transient nature and the futility of placing ultimate value on material possessions. Ecclesiastes 5:15 (NLT) captures this truth: *"We all come to the end of our lives as naked and empty-handed as on the day we were born. We can't take our riches with us."* In this cyclical reality of life beginning and ending with nothing nakedness becomes a powerful metaphor, urging us to focus on values that transcend physical wealth: spiritual growth, love, and humility. Doesn't this realization compel us to reconsider our priorities? Shouldn't we strive to build legacies rooted in faith and relationships rather than in transient wealth?

The story of Adam and Eve provides a foundational lesson in the simplicity of nakedness. Initially, their nakedness reflected their total dependence on God and their harmonious relationship with Him and creation. However, after their disobedience, nakedness became a source of shame, signifying a loss of innocence and self-reliance. This shift teaches us that true humility lies in acknowledging our dependence on God. As C.S. Lewis once wrote, *"Humility is not thinking less of yourself, but thinking of yourself less."* Nakedness, in its original context, invites us to shed the pride and pretense that distance us from God, embracing instead a life of simplicity and authenticity. Can we, like Adam and Eve before the fall, live with such vulnerability and reliance on God?

Jesus exemplified the humility symbolized by nakedness in His life and ministry. Philippians 2:7 (NLT) states, *"Instead, he gave up his divine privileges; he took the humble position of a slave and was born as a human being."* Jesus willingly set aside heavenly glory to embrace a life of simplicity, demonstrating that true greatness lies in servanthood and humility. His earthly life was devoid of material wealth, yet it was rich in purpose and love. This serves as a lesson for current and future generations: our worth is not measured by what we possess but by how we reflect Christ's character in our actions and relationships. Isn't Christ's example a call to let go of material attachments and seek eternal treasures?

For today's Christians, nakedness as a symbol of humility challenges societal norms that glorify wealth and status. In a culture that often equates success with accumulation, this symbolism reminds us to prioritize what truly matters faith, relationships, and integrity. The next generation can draw inspiration from biblical characters like Job, who, despite losing everything, declared, *"I came naked from my mother's womb, and I will be naked when I leave. The Lord gave me what I had, and the Lord has taken it away. Praise the name of the Lord!"* (Job 1:21, NLT). This unwavering trust in God underscores the enduring truth that our ultimate security rests in Him, not in earthly possessions.

Ultimately, nakedness as a reminder of simplicity and humility serves as a guiding principle for generations to come. It calls us to reframe our values and focus on what endures our relationship with God and the legacy of love and faith we leave behind. This perspective equips us to live with intentionality, resisting the distractions of materialism. How different would our lives be if we fully embraced this principle? Nakedness, far from being a symbol of lack, becomes a profound reminder of our dependence on God and our call to live humbly, authentically, and purposefully.

NAKEDNESS AS A CALL TO AUTHENTICITY

In presenting Adam and Eve to each other in their nakedness, God underscored the significance of living authentically. Their physical nakedness was more than an invitation to physical intimacy; it symbolized a deeper reality a call to complete openness and vulnerability. Genesis 2:25 (NLT) states, *"Now the man and his wife were both naked, but they felt no shame."* This unashamed state reflects a relationship built on trust, honesty, and transparency, where neither felt the need to hide or pretend. It's a profound reminder that authenticity is foundational to human connections. How often do we feel the need to wear masks, even in our closest relationships? Could we learn from Adam and Eve's initial openness to embrace who we truly are, free from the fear of judgment?

Nakedness as authenticity strengthens relationships by fostering trust and understanding. When Adam and Eve stood before each other without shame, it illustrated the depth of connection possible when individuals are genuine and vulnerable. Transparency eliminates the barriers that lead to miscommunication and misunderstanding. In modern relationships, particularly in marriage, authenticity allows partners to share their fears, dreams, and struggles, creating a bond that can withstand life's trials. As Christian author Henri Nouwen wrote, *"The friend who can be silent with us in a moment of despair or confusion, who can stay with us in an hour of grief and bereavement, who can tolerate not knowing, not healing, not curing, that is a friend who cares."* Authenticity invites such deep care and connection. Doesn't this challenge us to rethink how open we are in our relationships?

Furthermore, authenticity is essential for navigating challenges and fostering resilience. When couples are transparent about their feelings, struggles, and needs, they can face difficulties together, as a united team. Adam and Eve's eventual fall from grace highlights the devastating impact of hiding and blame-shifting, showing that authenticity must be sustained even in adversity. James 5:16 (NLT) advises, *"Confess your sins to each other and pray for each other so that you may be healed. The earnest prayer of a righteous person has great power and produces wonderful results."* This verse illustrates how openness, paired with humility, leads to healing and growth. Isn't it through such honesty that relationships can thrive and withstand life's storms?

Nakedness as a call to authenticity also has a spiritual dimension. Just as Adam and Eve were transparent with each other, God calls believers to be authentic in their relationship with Him. Pretending or hiding before God is futile, as Hebrews 4:13 (NLT) reminds us: *"Nothing in all creation is hidden from God. Everything is naked and exposed before his eyes, and he is the one to whom we are accountable."* Embracing this truth liberates us from pretense, allowing us to approach God with honesty about our struggles and imperfections. As A.W. Tozer observed, *"The man who comes to a right belief about God is relieved of ten thousand temporal problems."* Could this understanding transform how we relate to God and others, helping us live with integrity and peace?

For current and future generations, nakedness as a call to authenticity offers a timeless lesson. In a world increasingly dominated by curated social media personas and superficial interactions, the biblical principle of nakedness challenges us to prioritize genuine connections over appearances. Teaching younger generations, the value of authenticity equips them to build meaningful relationships and resist the pressures of societal pretense. It reminds them that their worth is not tied to what they show on the outside but to the truth of who they are as God's creation. How would our world change if authenticity became the norm, not the exception? By embracing this principle, individuals can reflect God's design for relationships, inspiring others to live lives marked by honesty, humility, and love.

NAKEDNESS AS A MESSAGE OF DIVINE PURPOSE

Nakedness in creation profoundly symbolizes humanity's divine purpose and focus on God's will. When God created Adam and Eve and placed them in the Garden of Eden, He presented them in their naked state to emphasize simplicity, purity, and vulnerability. Genesis 2:25 (NLT) states, *"Now the man and his wife were both naked, but they felt no shame."* This unashamed nakedness reflects a life aligned with God's design a life centered on obedience and purpose, not marred by fear or distraction. Adam and Eve were tasked with caring for the garden and living in harmony with creation, a calling that was unmarred by societal pressures or material pursuits. Could their nakedness, free of adornment or pretense, be a divine reminder that humanity's purpose lies not in what we accumulate but in living out God's plan for our lives?

Nakedness invites us to reflect on the importance of spiritual fulfillment over temporary achievements. Adam and Eve's initial state reminds us that true satisfaction does not come from material possessions or worldly accolades but from aligning our lives with God's purpose. As Jesus said in Matthew 6:33 (NLT), *"Seek the Kingdom of God above all else, and live righteously, and he will give you everything you need."* This verse underscores that pursuing God's purpose brings provision, peace, and fulfillment beyond what the world can offer. How often do we allow our focus to be distracted by the pursuit of fleeting success rather than eternal significance? Nakedness calls us back to simplicity and reliance on God's guidance.

Moreover, the symbolism of nakedness highlights humanity's dependency on God. Adam and Eve, in their natural state, had no means to clothe or protect themselves outside of God's provision. This dependency mirrors our need to rely on God's grace and direction in every aspect of our lives. Christian author A.W. Tozer once wrote, *"The man who has God for his treasure has all things in One."* Nakedness teaches us that our sufficiency is not found in ourselves but in God, who provides for our needs and equips us for His work. Does this not challenge us to relinquish control and trust God more deeply, recognizing that He alone is the source of our purpose and provision?

The message of nakedness also reminds us of the simplicity of living in harmony with God's creation. Adam and Eve's responsibilities in the Garden of Eden were straightforward they were to cultivate the earth and steward its resources. This simplicity reflects the ease of a life lived according to God's purpose, unburdened by the complications of sin and worldly ambitions. Nakedness invites us to consider how we can return to this simplicity by focusing on our spiritual purpose and stewardship rather than accumulating possessions or striving for status. Could embracing this perspective transform the way we live and interact with others, fostering contentment and a sense of divine mission?

For current and future generations, nakedness as a message of divine purpose offers a timeless lesson about priorities, reliance on God, and simplicity. In a society obsessed with external appearances and material success, this message encourages a counterculturalapproach one that values spiritual growth, authenticity, and alignment with God's will. Teaching this truth to future generations equips them to find lasting fulfilment, free from the pressures of comparison and consumerism. How might the world change if more people embraced this perspective? By understanding the deeper meaning of nakedness, individuals can live lives marked by purpose, contentment, and an unwavering focus on the eternal, inspiring others to do the same.

NOTE THESE

Integrity Requires Transparency – Living with integrity means being open and honest in all areas of life, fostering trust and accountability.

Openness Strengthens Relationships – Transparency in marriage and friendships creates a foundation of trust, allowing individuals to be fully known and loved.

Authenticity Before God is Essential – Spiritual integrity involves being honest with God about our struggles, as nothing is hidden from Him.

Simplicity and Humility Lead to True Fulfilment – Nakedness symbolizes a life free from material distractions, emphasizing dependence on God rather than possessions.

Vulnerability Promotes Growth and Healing – Being open about weaknesses allows for restoration, both in relationships and in our spiritual journey.

CHAPTER FIVE

Nakedness as an Invitation to Approach God Openly

Nakedness in the Garden of Eden signifies a profound truth: it is an invitation to approach God with honesty, sincerity, and vulnerability. Adam and Eve, standing before God without shame, reflect an unbroken relationship free from sin's distortions. Their physical nakedness represented spiritual openness nothing was hidden from their Creator, and their communion with Him was unhindered. This symbolizes the transparency God desires in our relationship with Him. Are we not reminded in Hebrews 4:13 (NIV) that *"nothing in all creation is hidden from God's sight. Everything is uncovered and laid bare before the eyes of him to whom we must give account"*? This verse emphasizes the futility of hiding from God and the freedom that comes from approaching Him with authenticity.

Spiritual nakedness becomes a call to remove the masks and pretenses that often define our daily lives. In Matthew 11:28-29 (NIV), Jesus invites us, saying, *"Come to me, all you who are weary and burdened, and I will give you rest. Take my yoke upon you and learn from me, for I am gentle and humble in heart, and you will find rest for your souls."* This invitation is a reminder that God does not expect perfection but openness. When we come to Him in our true state flawed, weary, and burdened we experience His grace and renewal. How often do we try to present a polished version of ourselves, fearing rejection? Nakedness before God reassures us that we are fully known and fully loved, even in our brokenness.

By embracing this spiritual nakedness, we open the door to transformation. Just as a sculptor cannot mold a hidden or covered block of clay, God works most effectively when we expose our hearts to Him. Christian author Max Lucado writes, *"God loves you just the way you are, but He refuses to leave you that way. He wants you to be just like Jesus."* Approaching God without barriers allows Him to shape us into His image, refining our character and deepening our faith. This process requires trust, trust that God sees the depths of our hearts and still chooses to work through us for His glory. Do we truly believe that His grace is sufficient, even when we lay bare our failures and struggles?

Nakedness before God also fosters a deeper sense of intimacy in our relationship with Him. Transparency invites closeness, and as we open ourselves to God, we experience the joy of His presence. Psalm 34:18 (NIV) assures us, *"The Lord is close to the brokenhearted and saves those who are crushed in spirit."* This closeness is not reserved for the strong or perfect but for those willing to approach God honestly. When we shed the barriers of pride and self-sufficiency, we find that God meets us in our vulnerability, offering peace, guidance, and a deeper awareness of His love. How might our spiritual lives change if we consistently approach God with this level of openness?

For our generations, the lesson of nakedness as an invitation to approach God openly is transformative. In a world that often celebrates appearances and discourages vulnerability, this principle challenges us to prioritize authenticity over image. By teaching this truth, we equip future generations to find freedom in God's unconditional love and to build their faith on a foundation of honesty and trust. Can there be a more profound legacy than passing on the courage to live transparently before God and others? Nakedness as a symbol of openness encourages us all to embrace our true selves, lean into God's grace, and live with the assurance that His love is greater than our imperfections.

NAKEDNESS AS A REMINDER OF LIFE'S TRANSIENCE AND THE FUTILITY OF MATERIALISM

The imagery of nakedness at birth and death is a powerful reminder of the brevity of human life and the futility of materialism. Ecclesiastes 5:15 (NIV) states, *"Everyone comes naked from their mother's womb, and as everyone comes, so they depart. They take nothing from their toil that they can carry in their hands."* This verse pinpoints the truth that we enter the world with nothing and leave with nothing, emphasizing that material possessions are temporary and cannot be carried into eternity. Nakedness serves as a metaphor for life's transient nature, prompting us to reflect on the futility of placing too much value on wealth and worldly success. Is it not sobering to consider that all our earthly gains will ultimately remain behind when we depart this life?

Job's declaration in Job 1:21 (NIV) *"Naked I came from my mother's womb, and naked I shall depart. The Lord gave, and the Lord has taken away; blessed be the name of the Lord"* adds depth to this reflection. Job's words express not only acceptance of life's impermanence but also a recognition of God's sovereignty. Nakedness here symbolizes the humility of recognizing that everything we have, from possessions to life itself, is a gift from God. How often do we pause to acknowledge that all we own is temporary, entrusted to us for stewardship rather than possession? Nakedness calls us back to this humility, reminding us to align our priorities with God's eternal purposes.

Material possessions, though often seen as symbols of success, can become burdens that distract us from spiritual growth. Christian author Randy Alcorn writes, *"You can't take it with you, but you can send it on ahead."* This perspective invites us to invest in eternal treasures acts of love, generosity, and faithfulness that align with God's kingdom. Nakedness at birth and death challenges us to view life through a spiritual lens, evaluating our actions and values in light of eternity. Do our daily pursuits reflect this eternal perspective, or are we caught in the cycle of accumulating what we cannot keep?

This understanding of nakedness serves as a lesson for both current and future generations. In a world increasingly driven by consumerism and material wealth, the symbolism of nakedness reminds us to focus on what truly matters: our relationship with God, our character, and the legacy of love and faith we leave behind. Jesus Himself warned in Matthew 6:19-20 (NIV), *"Do not store up for yourselves treasures on earth, where moths and vermin destroy, and where thieves break in and steal. But store up for yourselves treasures in heaven, where moths and vermin do not destroy, and where thieves do not break in and steal."* Nakedness invites us to embrace this perspective, prioritizing the eternal over the temporal.

For future generations, this message provides a foundation for living with purpose and intention. By understanding the transience of life, they can be encouraged to invest in relationships, community, and spiritual growth rather than chasing material wealth. Nakedness reminds us all that our true worth is found not in possessions but in our identity as children of God. As we teach this truth, we empower others to live with contentment, humility, and a focus on eternity, ensuring that their lives bear fruit that lasts far beyond their time on earth.

NAKEDNESS AND THE FUTILITY OF WEALTH

Nakedness powerfully illustrates the transience of material wealth, reminding us that earthly riches have no lasting value beyond this life. At birth, we arrive in the world with nothing, and at death, we leave in the same way. This reality serves as a humbling reminder that wealth, possessions, and achievements no matter how great are temporary. Nakedness symbolizes the futility of attaching our identity or purpose to material things. Jesus highlighted this truth when He asked, *"What good will it be for someone to gain the whole world, yet forfeit their soul?"* (Matthew 16:26, NIV). Does wealth truly provide the security and meaning we seek, or does it distract us from pursuing what truly matters?

King Solomon, despite his unparalleled wealth and wisdom, understood the fleeting nature of riches. In Ecclesiastes 5:15 (NIV), he states, "Everyone comes naked from their mother's womb, and as everyone comes, so they depart. They take nothing from their toil that they can carry in their hands." Solomon's reflections reveal that the pursuit of wealth is often a striving after wind—futile and without lasting fulfillment. How often do people sacrifice their time, health, and relationships for wealth, only to realize too late that these pursuits cannot satisfy the deeper longings of the heart? Nakedness forces us to confront this sobering truth and recalibrate our priorities.

The parable of the rich fool in Luke 12:16-21 further emphasizes this lesson. The man hoards wealth, building larger barns to store his surplus grain, only to die suddenly, leaving his possessions behind. God calls him a fool, saying, *"This is how it will be with whoever stores up things for themselves but is not rich toward God"* (Luke 12:21, NIV). Nakedness reminds us that life is fragile and uncertain; no amount of wealth can secure our future or define our worth. Are we, like the rich fool, accumulating wealth without considering how to be *"rich toward God"*? *Christian author John Piper writes, "The danger of riches is that they can lure us into a false security and a deceptive sense of independence from God."* Nakedness strips away that illusion, exposing the emptiness of wealth when disconnected from a life centered on God. Instead of hoarding possessions, nakedness invites us to invest in eternal treasures acts of generosity, faith, and love that cannot be lost or destroyed. Are we living as stewards of God's blessings, or are we clinging to wealth as if it were the source of our identity and security?

This understanding of nakedness serves as a timeless lesson for current and future generations, urging them to resist the cultural obsession with materialism and focus on what endures. It challenges us to teach children the value of contentment, gratitude, and spiritual richness over the fleeting allure of wealth. Nakedness, as a metaphor for life's transience, calls each generation to reevaluate their pursuits, embrace humility, and prioritize their relationship with God and others. In doing so, we leave behind not just an inheritance of material possessions but a legacy of faith and values that transcends time.

NAKEDNESS AS A POSTURE OF HUMILITY AND TRUST IN GOD'S SOVEREIGN WILL

The concept of nakedness in the Bible signifies human vulnerability and a deep sense of dependence on God. At its core, nakedness in Scripture is not just about physical exposure but a symbolic representation of our complete reliance on the Creator. The imagery of nakedness reminds us that we come into the world with nothing and leave with nothing, and that our very existence is a gift from God. Job, in the midst of unspeakable loss, encapsulates this understanding with his powerful words in Job 1:21 (NIV): *"Naked I came from my mother's womb, and naked I shall return there. The Lord gave, and the Lord has taken away; may the name of the Lord be praised."* Job's response is one of profound humility and trust, acknowledging that everything he had, from his family to his health, was given by God and could be taken away according to His sovereign will. Job's nakedness both literal and spiritual served as a posture of submission to God's will, teaching us how to approach life's hardships with unwavering faith.

This declaration of nakedness in the face of suffering teaches us an important lesson about humility. Job's understanding of his vulnerability, and his ability to submit to God's will, offers a model of faith that can be applied to our own lives. Do we, like Job, recognize that everything we have our wealth, health, relationships, and even life itself are gifts from God? When we lose something dear to us, are we quick to grumble, or can we, like Job, acknowledge that God is sovereign over all things? Job's words serve as a reminder that our possessions, status, and circumstances do not define us. It is God's will and purposes that give our lives true meaning and significance, not the temporary things we accumulate or enjoy.

The posture of nakedness before God challenges us to confront our attachment to the material world. In our consumer-driven society, we are often led to believe that possessions, success, and comfort are the ultimate goals in life. However, nakedness before God reminds us of the futility of finding our security in anything other than Him. Jesus cautioned against storing up treasures on earth in Matthew 6:19-21 (NIV), saying, *"Do not store up for yourselves treasures on earth, where moths and vermin destroy, and where thieves break in and steal. But store up for yourselves treasures in heaven, where moths and vermin do not destroy, and where thieves do not break in and steal."* Jesus emphasizes that the things of this world are fleeting, and our ultimate trust must be placed in God's eternal promises, not in material wealth or achievements.

Christian author A.W. Tozer once wrote, *"The way to deeper life lies through surrender, not through achievement."* This quote underscores the importance of surrendering to God's sovereignty in every aspect of our lives. Just as Job demonstrated that his trust was in God's will, not in his wealth or health, we too are called to surrender our desires, ambitions, and possessions to the Lord. Nakedness, in this sense, is a powerful reminder to let go of our need for control and recognize that God is sovereign. Our identity, value, and ultimate security rest not in what we possess or accomplish, but in whose we are His beloved children, held in His sovereign care.

This teaching on nakedness as a posture of humility and trust in God's will serves as an invaluable lesson for current and future generations. In a world that often promotes self-reliance, achievement, and accumulation, this biblical perspective calls us to examine our hearts and shift our focus from the temporary to the eternal. As we learn to trust God with our possessions, relationships, and circumstances, we cultivate a deeper reliance on His sovereignty, which strengthens our faith in His perfect plan. For the generations to come, this understanding will guide them to value humility over pride, contentment over materialism, and faith over fear. Nakedness before God teaches us that we are not the architects of our own lives; instead, we are called to live in humble submission to the One who holds our lives in His hands.

NAKEDNESS AND THE CALL TO ETERNAL PERSPECTIVE

The imagery of nakedness at birth and death serves as a poignant reminder of the fleeting nature of our earthly lives and the impermanence of material possessions. From the moment of birth, we come into the world with nothing, and as we depart from this world, we take nothing with us. The cycle of nakedness reminds us that wealth, achievements, and status are temporary and do not accompany us into eternity. Ecclesiastes 5:16 (NIV) highlights this truth when Solomon asks, *"As everyone comes, so they depart, and what do they gain, since they toil for the wind?"* This rhetorical question exposes the emptiness of worldly pursuits, encouraging us to focus on what has eternal value. Solomon's words challenge us to reconsider what we prioritize in life, reminding us that everything we amass in this world will ultimately fade away.

In this context, nakedness symbolizes more than just physical vulnerability it represents spiritual clarity. It calls us to examine our lives and assess whether we are focused on pursuits that have lasting significance. Are we living for temporary success, wealth, or recognition, or are we building treasures that last beyond this life? Jesus' teaching in Matthew 6:19-20 (NIV) resonates with this message: *"Do not store up for yourselves treasures on earth, where moths and vermin destroy, and where thieves break in and steal. But store up for yourselves treasures in heaven, where moths and vermin do not destroy, and where thieves do not break in and steal."* These verses remind us that the things of this world are perishable, and true value is found in the eternal our relationship with God, acts of love, and living in alignment with His will.

Nakedness, in this sense, challenges us to adopt an eternal perspective. It encourages us to look beyond the immediate and temporary concerns of life and focus on what truly matters in the grand scope of eternity. In a culture where success is often defined by material wealth, accomplishments, and status, the metaphor of nakedness invites us to shift our focus toward spiritual growth and alignment with God's purposes. In the book of Colossians, Paul urges believers to set their minds on things above, saying, *"Since, then, you have been raised with Christ, set your hearts on things above, where Christ is, seated at the right hand of God"* (Colossians 3:1-2, NIV). This call to focus on the eternal reminds us that our worth and purpose are not found in the things we possess but in our identity as children of God.

Christian author C.S. Lewis once wrote, *"Aim at Heaven and you will get Earth 'thrown in': aim at Earth and you will get neither."* This profound quote reinforces the concept that when we prioritize eternal goals, the blessings of this life are naturally added to us. Nakedness, as a symbol of humility and clarity, invites us to reassess our goals and motivations. Are we so caught up in the pursuit of success and material possessions that we lose sight of the eternal purpose for which we were created? Nakedness, therefore, serves as a wake-up call to examine whether our lives reflect the priorities that align with God's eternal kingdom or whether we are chasing after the temporary things that Solomon describes as "toiling for the wind."

This perspective on nakedness challenges both current and future generations to live intentionally, with an awareness of the fleeting nature of life and the true value of eternal pursuits. In a world that constantly emphasizes material success and personal achievements, the biblical call to embrace a naked, eternal perspective provides a much-needed counterpoint. The lessons learned from this perspective will inspire future generations to live with purpose and focus on the things that will endure forever faith, love, integrity, and service. As we embrace this call to eternal perspective, we will be better equipped to navigate the pressures of the world, ensuring that our lives reflect the values of God's kingdom and our lasting inheritance in Him.

CHAPTER SIX

NAKEDNESS AS THE ULTIMATE SPIRITUAL LESSON

The imagery of nakedness in Scripture serves as a significant spiritual lesson about human frailty and our absolute dependence on God. Nakedness, in its most literal sense, exposes us, leaving us without any protective barriers or defenses. This vulnerability reveals our true state before God one of complete reliance on His provision. As humans, we often cling to the illusion of self-sufficiency, believing that we can navigate life through our own strength or resources. Yet, nakedness reminds us that we are not self-made or independent. Everything we have, from our breath to our abilities, is a gift from God. James 1:17 (NIV) reinforces this truth: *"Every good and perfect gift is from above, coming down from the Father of the heavenly lights."* This verse emphasizes that all we possess comes from God, underscoring our dependency on Him for every aspect of life.

In the Genesis creation narrative, Adam and Eve's initial state of nakedness symbolizes their unbroken relationship with God, where they were fully reliant on Him for their identity and sustenance. They lived in a state of innocence, unashamed of their vulnerability because they were completely secure in God's provision. Genesis 2:25 (NIV) notes, *"Adam and his wife were both naked, and they felt no shame."* This unashamed nakedness illustrates the purity of their relationship with God before the fall. They were free to be fully themselves without the fear of judgment or rejection, because their identity and worth were rooted in their Creator. This state of nakedness, free from shame, was the ideal, reflecting a harmonious relationship where they were both spiritually and physically vulnerable, yet fully cared for by God.

However, after sin entered the world, Adam and Eve's nakedness became associated with shame and vulnerability. Genesis 3:7 (NIV) states, *"Then the eyes of both of them were opened, and they realized they were naked; so they sewed fig leaves together and made themselves loincloths."* The awareness of their nakedness came with a sense of guilt and fear, illustrating how sin disrupts our relationship with God. Instead of embracing their vulnerability as a gift from God, they attempted to cover up their insufficiency through their own means. This act of covering themselves symbolizes the human tendency to hide our weaknesses and failings rather than surrendering them to God. Sin introduces the false notion that we must hide our true selves to be accepted, but God's grace invites us to return to a place of honest vulnerability, trusting in His provision for our lives.

Christian author A.W. Tozer wrote, *"The person who has truly surrendered to Christ will be willing to let go of all self-reliance."* This quote aligns with the spiritual lesson embedded in the concept of nakedness. It challenges us to relinquish the illusion of control and self-sufficiency and to trust in God's sovereign grace for our daily needs and spiritual security. For current and future generations, this understanding of nakedness as a symbol of complete dependence on God provides a powerful lesson in humility. It teaches us that we do not have to hide our imperfections or attempt to live independently of God. Instead, we are called to live with a posture of vulnerability before Him, recognizing that His grace is sufficient to cover our weaknesses and guide us through life's challenges. By embracing this truth, we can cultivate a deeper trust in God's provision and experience the freedom that comes from relying fully on Him.

NAKEDNESS: STRIPS AWAY ILLUSIONS OF SELF-SUFFICIENCY

Nakedness, as portrayed in Scripture, strips away the illusions of self-sufficiency and reveals the profound truth of human dependence on God. Job's experience after losing everything is a powerful example of this spiritual reality. In Job 1:21 (NIV), he declares, *"Naked I came from my mother's womb, and naked I shall return there. The Lord gave, and the Lord has taken away; blessed be the name of the Lord."* Job's acknowledgement of his nakedness is not just about the loss of material possessions, but about a deeper recognition that everything he had his wealth, health, and family was given by God. Job's response shows that he understood his dependence on God for his very existence. In the face of overwhelming loss, he was not consumed by despair but instead trusted in God's sovereignty. His nakedness symbolizes the stripping away of any illusions of self-reliance, and he chose to trust in God's will, even in hardship.

Similarly, Solomon, in the book of Ecclesiastes, delves into the futility of placing our trust in material wealth or human effort. In Ecclesiastes 5:15 (NIV), he writes, *"As everyone comes, so they depart, and what do they gain, since they toil for the wind?"* Solomon, despite his immense wealth and wisdom, understood that life's meaning is not found in possessions or accomplishments, but in a relationship with God. He recognized that material wealth is transient and ultimately meaningless if it is pursued apart from God. Solomon's reflections echo the message that nakedness, as a symbol, represents the removal of false securities and distractions. Just as we enter this world naked, without material possessions, we will leave with nothing. This calls us to reconsider what we value and where we place our trust.

The example of both Job and Solomon teaches us a critical lesson about human vulnerability and dependence on God. How often do we try to build our identity around our possessions, achievements, or status? The reality of nakedness, both literal and metaphorical, reminds us that we can't take any of these with us. What truly matters is our relationship with God, which is eternal. The world encourages self-sufficiency and the accumulation of wealth as signs of success, but Scripture teaches that apart from God, we have nothing of lasting value. This truth should challenge us to ask: Are we relying on our own abilities and possessions to secure our future, or are we trusting in God's provision and purpose for our lives?

For current and future generations, the lesson of nakedness as a symbol of vulnerability and dependence on God serves as a call to humility and trust in the sovereignty of God. In a world that often emphasizes self-reliance and material success, it is essential to remember that everything we have is a gift from God. Nakedness teaches us that we are not in control, and our ultimate security lies not in what we possess, but in the one who provides for us. As we embrace this truth, we are called to live lives of gratitude, humility, and trust in God's plan, understanding that He is our true source of meaning and fulfilment, both now and for eternity.

NAKEDNESS: REMINDER OF OUR NEEDS FOR GOD'S GRACE AND PRESENCE

Nakedness, as portrayed in Scripture, serves as a profound reminder of our deep need for God's grace and presence in our lives. From the beginning, when Adam and Eve were created, they were naked and unashamed, symbolizing their innocence and pure dependence on God. However, once sin entered the world, their nakedness became a symbol of vulnerability and separation from God. In Genesis 3:6-7 (NIV), after Adam and Eve ate the forbidden fruit, their eyes were opened, and they realized their nakedness, which led them to cover themselves with fig leaves. This act of covering themselves revealed their newfound awareness of sin and their need for God's grace. Their nakedness, once a symbol of innocence, now represented their brokenness and their need for God's intervention to restore the relationship that had been fractured by sin.

The state of nakedness, especially in the context of Adam and Eve's story, underscores the fact that humanity is inherently vulnerable and cannot stand in its own strength. Without God's grace, humanity is exposed and helpless, unable to hide or cover its sin. As Paul writes in Romans 3:23 (NIV), *"for all have sinned and fall short of the glory of God."* Just as Adam and Eve could not cover their shame without God's help, we, too, are incapable of covering our sins or providing for our deepest needs apart from God's grace. This truth invites us to acknowledge our own vulnerabilities and our dependence on God to meet our spiritual, emotional, and physical needs. It reminds us that without God's presence, we are like the prodigal son who found himself destitute and lost, yearning for the embrace of his father (Luke 15:17-24).

Furthermore, nakedness reveals not only our dependence on God's grace but also our need for His continual presence in our lives. In Exodus 33:14 (NIV), God tells Moses, *"My Presence will go with you, and I will give you rest."* The Israelites were reminded time and again that they could not face the challenges of life without God's guidance and presence. Nakedness, in this context, symbolizes more than just our physical need it is a spiritual cry for God to be with us, to guide us, and to sustain us. Just as a child cannot survive without the constant presence and care of a parent, we, too, must live in the continual awareness of God's presence in our lives. It is through this dependence on God's grace and presence that we find strength, wisdom, and peace.

The lesson of nakedness as a reminder of our need for God's grace and presence is essential for both current and future generations. In a world that often celebrates self-sufficiency and independence, nakedness calls us to humility, recognizing that we are nothing apart from God. It challenges us to live with a constant awareness of our dependence on Him and to seek His grace in every moment of life. The question we must ask ourselves is: Are we living as if we can face life without God, or are we daily acknowledging our need for His grace and presence? For the generations to come, this lesson will serve as a foundation for living lives that are fully surrendered to God, trusting in

His provision, guidance, and love. It teaches us that we are not meant to journey through life alone, but in the constant embrace of God's grace and presence.

NAKEDNESS AS A REFLECTION OF OUR BEGINNING AND END

Nakedness, as presented in Scripture, serves as a powerful reflection of both our beginning and end, reminding us of the fleeting nature of our lives and the unchanging nature of God's purpose for humanity. At the beginning of creation, when Adam and Eve were first formed, their nakedness was a sign of their purity, innocence, and unbroken communion with God. In Genesis 2:25 (NIV), it says, *"Adam and his wife were both naked, and they felt no shame."* Their nakedness was not a symbol of vulnerability or sin, but rather a reflection of their divine purpose: to live in harmony with God and with one another. It was a state of perfect openness, both physically and spiritually, where there was no shame, fear, or need for hiding. This pure state of nakedness at creation highlights our original design and intended relationship with God.

However, as sin entered the world, nakedness transformed into a symbol of vulnerability and shame. When Adam and Eve disobeyed God, their nakedness became a reminder of their brokenness and the separation that sin brought between humanity and God. In Genesis 3:6-7 (NIV), after they ate the forbidden fruit, *"the eyes of both of them were opened, and they realized they were naked; so they sewed fig leaves together and made themselves loincloths."* Their awareness of their nakedness marked the fall of mankind a tragic shift from innocence to the realization of guilt and separation from God. This transformation serves as a reminder that our relationship with God, originally pure and unhindered, was fractured by sin. Nakedness, in this sense, becomes a reflection of the loss of the intimacy that humanity once shared with God.

As we reflect on nakedness in the context of both our beginning and end, we are reminded of our mortality. In Ecclesiastes 5:15 (NIV), Solomon writes, *"Everyone comes naked from their mother's womb, and as everyone comes, so they depart."* Our entrance into the world is marked by nakedness, and so too is our departure. This cyclical nature of life, coming into the world with nothing and leaving with nothing, underscores the transient nature of earthly possessions, status, and achievements. As we reflect on the brevity of life and our eventual return to the earth, we are reminded of the futility of accumulating wealth or placing our identity in temporal things. In the words of Christian author John Wesley, *"The world is a stage; we are merely players. Our lives have an appointed beginning and end."* Nakedness, as a reflection of both our beginning and end, calls us to shift our focus from the fleeting things of this world to the eternal purposes of God.

Ultimately, the lesson of nakedness as a reflection of our beginning and end calls us to live with an eternal perspective. We are reminded that our earthly lives are short and temporary, and our ultimate hope lies in our relationship with God. As Paul writes in 1 Timothy 6:7 (NIV), *"For we brought nothing into the world, and we can take nothing out of it."* This awareness of our humble beginnings and inevitable end should lead us to focus on what truly matters our spiritual growth, our relationship with God, and our service to others. For current and future generations, this message serves as a reminder to live with purpose and to seek after eternal treasures, rather than being consumed by the pursuit of temporary gains. Nakedness, as both a beginning and an end, teaches us humility, dependence on God, and the importance of investing in what truly lasts our souls, our relationships, and our eternal destiny.

NAKEDNESS AS AN ACKNOWLEDGEMENT OF GOD'S SOVEREIGNTY

Nakedness, in both its literal and symbolic sense, represents a deep acknowledgement of God's sovereignty over all aspects of our lives. From the moment we are born, we come into the world with nothing, a stark reminder that our existence is entirely dependent on God. In 1 Timothy 6:7 (NIV), Paul writes, *"For we brought nothing into the world, and we can take nothing out of it."* This passage underscores the futility of clinging to material wealth or achievements, as they hold no eternal value. Our physical nakedness at birth reminds us of our inherent vulnerability and dependence on God's grace, a condition that continues throughout our lives. In the face of life's impermanence, acknowledging our nakedness serves as an expression of humility, where we surrender ourselves to God's will, recognizing that everything we have, including life itself, is a gift from Him.

This theme is also echoed in the life of Job, who, after experiencing profound loss, acknowledges that his life and possessions are entirely at God's discretion. In Job 1:21 (NIV), he says, *"Naked I came from my mother's womb, and naked I shall return there. The Lord gave, and the Lord has taken away; blessed be the name of the Lord."* Job's recognition of his nakedness reflects his understanding of God's ultimate sovereignty, even in the face of suffering. By surrendering his grief and loss to God's will, Job exemplifies a posture of trust and humility. This acknowledgement of God's sovereignty is not just about accepting blessings but also about trusting God through trials and difficulties. Job's surrender teaches us that nakedness is a symbol of offering everything our wealth, health, relationships, and dreams into God's hands, knowing that He is the one who ordains our steps.

King David, too, echoes this acknowledgement of God's sovereign rule in Psalm 24:1 (NIV), where he writes, *"The earth is the Lord's, and everything in it, the world, and all who live in it."* This declaration of God's ownership over all creation calls us to see ourselves as stewards rather than owners. Nakedness, in this sense, becomes a metaphor for stewardship, where we hold everything loosely, understanding that all things ultimately belong to God. Whether it is our material possessions, our talents, or our relationships, everything is entrusted to us by God to use for His glory. The concept of nakedness challenges us to evaluate our attachment to the things of this world, reminding us that they are temporary and should not take precedence over our relationship with God. Are we honoring God with the resources He has entrusted to us, or are we hoarding them for our own selfish gain?

In times of suffering and loss, as demonstrated by Job, we are called to adopt a mindset of surrender to God's sovereign will. Job's statement in Job 2:10 (NIV), "Shall we accept good from God, and not trouble?" challenges us to reconsider how we respond to life's challenges. It is easy to praise God in times of prosperity, but can we maintain that same trust when life brings us pain and hardship? Nakedness, as a symbol of surrender, invites us to release our own understanding and trust in God's wisdom, especially when life doesn't make sense. Proverbs 3:5-6 (NIV) encourages this perspective, saying, *"Trust in the Lord with all your heart and lean not on your own understanding; in all your ways submit to Him, and He will make your paths straight."* This passage teaches us that surrendering to God's plan, especially in moments of uncertainty, will lead to peace and direction, even when we don't have all the answers.

The ultimate lesson of nakedness as an acknowledgement of God's sovereignty and surrender is that we are called to live lives of humility, trust, and dependence on God. In a world where self-sufficiency and independence are often idolized, the metaphor of nakedness reminds us that we are not in control of our lives God is. For both current and future generations, this message serves as a timeless lesson on the importance of surrendering everything to God, whether in moments of abundance or hardship. It challenges us to shift our focus from worldly pursuits to eternal perspectives, trusting that God's will is always for our good, and that His purposes will prevail in our lives. As we embrace the truth of our nakedness, we learn to live in the freedom of surrender, allowing God to shape our lives according to His sovereign plan.

NAKEDNESS AND GRATITUDE FOR LIFE'S BLESSINGS

Nakedness teaches us to hold material possessions lightly and use them wisely, focusing on eternal purposes. The concept of nakedness reminds us of the fleeting nature of material possessions. As Job observed, *"Naked I came from my mother's womb, and naked I shall return there. The Lord gave, and the Lord has taken away; blessed be the name of the Lord"* (Job 1:21). This statement reflects Job's deep understanding that everything he possessed—his wealth, family, and status—was a temporary gift from God. Nakedness, as a metaphor, calls us to view our possessions as tools to glorify God and serve others rather than as ends in themselves.

Acknowledging that we enter and leave this world with nothing fosters a heart of gratitude. Instead of clinging to material wealth, nakedness encourages us to thank God for His provision and to steward His gifts with care. Solomon's reflections in Ecclesiastes 5:19 reinforce this perspective: *"When God gives someone wealth and possessions, and the ability to enjoy them, to accept their lot and be happy in their toil—this is a gift of God."* Nakedness teaches us to appreciate the blessings of life while recognizing their temporary nature. The Bible warns against the dangers of greed and the futility of storing up earthly treasures. Jesus Himself taught in Matthew 6:19-21, *"Do not store up for yourselves treasures on earth, where moths and vermin destroy, and where thieves break in and steal. But store up for yourselves treasures in heaven... For where your treasure is, there your heart will be also."* Nakedness as a metaphor, challenges us to detach from greed, which often leads to dissatisfaction and misuse of God's blessings. Instead, it directs us to focus on eternal purposes, aligning our lives with God's priorities.

Nakedness also reminds us of our responsibility to use our resources for good. Paul's instructions in 1 Timothy 6:17-18 highlight this call: *"Command those who are rich in this present world not to be arrogant nor to put their hope in wealth, which is so uncertain, but to put their hope in God... Command them to do good, to be rich in good deeds, and to be generous and willing to share."* By holding possessions lightly, we can live generously, using our blessings to uplift others and advance God's kingdom.

Nakedness underscores the truth that our ultimate purpose transcends material wealth. As Solomon wisely noted in Ecclesiastes 5:15, *"Everyone comes naked from their mother's womb, and as everyone comes, so they depart. They take nothing from their toil that they can carry in their hands."* This perspective encourages us to focus on eternal values—love, faith, and service—rather than the accumulation of possessions.

NAKEDNESS IN WORSHIP AND ITS CONTROVERSIES

Some modern interpretations of nakedness in worship reflect an attempt to return to the original state of creation, but they also invite reflection on deeper spiritual meanings. The concept of nakedness in worship has been explored in some modern practices, where physical nakedness is embraced as a symbol of purity and transparency before God. This controversial practice seeks to emulate the state of Adam and Eve before the Fall, when they were naked and unashamed in the presence of God (Genesis 2:25). The proponents of such practices believe that by removing physical coverings, they symbolize their spiritual openness and humility before God. While this approach is rare and met with varying degrees of acceptance, it raises an important question: what does God truly desire from us in worship?

The Bible emphasizes that God looks beyond outward appearances to the condition of the heart. In 1 Samuel 16:7, NIV, God declares, *"The Lord does not look at the things people look at. People look at the outward appearance, but the Lord looks at the heart."* Physical nakedness is not a requirement for worship, but spiritual nakedness a posture of honesty, vulnerability, and openness is essential. This spiritual nakedness aligns with Jesus' teaching in John 4:24, where He says, *"God is spirit, and His worshipers must worship in the Spirit and in truth."*

The practice of physical nakedness in worship pinpoints a longing for humility and sincerity. However, it is crucial to distinguish between symbolic acts and the true nature of worship. Micah 6:8, NIV captures the essence of what God desires: *"To act justly and to love mercy and to walk humbly with your God."* True worship involves surrendering our pride, acknowledging our dependence on God, and approaching Him with genuine hearts, rather than focusing on external symbols.

While some interpret physical nakedness in worship as a return to innocence, others question its appropriateness and theological soundness.

Paul addresses similar concerns in 1 Corinthians 14:40, NIV, advising that *"everything should be done in a fitting and orderly way."* Worship practices should foster reverence and unity, avoiding actions that might cause confusion or division within the body of Christ. The emphasis should remain on the spiritual principles of worship rather than the physical expressions.

The deeper lesson of nakedness lies in its symbolism of transparency before God. In Hebrews 4:13, NIV, the writer reminds us, *"Nothing in all creation is hidden from God's sight. Everything is uncovered and laid bare before the eyes of Him to whom we must give account."* This verse captures the essence of spiritual nakedness an acknowledgement that God sees and knows everything about us, and our response should be to approach Him with honesty and reverence.

NAKEDNESS AS A SYMBOL OF PURITY AND SINCERITY

The concept of nakedness often symbolizes purity and transparency, representing an unhidden state before God. While physical expressions like wearing simple garments or avoiding adornments aim to convey this spiritual truth, the Bible emphasizes that what God truly seeks is the condition of the heart. In Isaiah 29:13, NIV, the Lord declares, *"These people come near to me with their mouth and honor me with their lips, but their hearts are far from me. Their worship of me is based on merely human rules they have been taught."* This passage reminds us that external acts of devotion must align with internal sincerity for our worship to be genuine.

Many religious traditions associate outward simplicity, such as modest dress or abstaining from luxury, with inner holiness. For example, groups like the "Church of Holiness" advocate for modesty and a rejection of worldly distractions as symbolic acts of purity. These practices stem from a desire to emulate spiritual nakedness an openness to God's will and a rejection of pride or materialism. The Apostle Paul similarly instructs in 1 Timothy 2:9-10, *"I also want the women to dress modestly, with decency and propriety, adorning themselves, not with elaborate hairstyles or gold or pearls or expensive clothes, but with good deeds, appropriate for women who profess to worship God."* Here, Paul emphasizes that good deeds and a pure heart hold more value in God's eyes than external appearances. While outward practices can serve as reminders of spiritual truths, they are not a substitute for genuine humility and transparency before God. Nakedness in this context symbolizes approaching God with a heart stripped of pretenses, pride, or self-reliance. As David prays in Psalm 51:10 NIV, *"Create in me a clean heart, O God, and renew a right spirit within me."* This plea illustrates that spiritual nakedness requires confessing our flaws and seeking transformation from within.

Consider two worshipers: one meticulously follows every outward ritual, dressing modestly and participating in every ceremony, yet harbors resentment and pride. The other comes before God in humility, confessing their weaknesses and seeking His guidance, even if they do not outwardly conform to all traditions. While the first may appear more devout, it is the second who embodies true nakedness before God. As Jesus teaches in Matthew 5:8, NIV, *"Blessed are the pure in heart, for they will see God."* Purity of heart, not external conformity, is the foundation of a sincere relationship with God. The ultimate lesson of nakedness is that God desires a relationship built on honesty and sincerity. Hebrews 4:13 reminds us, *"Nothing in all creation is hidden from God's sight. Everything is uncovered and laid bare before the eyes of Him to whom we must give account."* When we approach God with an open heart, acknowledging our dependence on Him and seeking His will, we embody the spiritual nakedness that reflects purity and sincerity.

NOTE THESE

Material possessions are temporary – We enter and leave the world with nothing, so we should not cling to wealth but use it wisely.

Gratitude leads to contentment – Recognizing that all blessings come from God helps us appreciate and steward them well.

True worship is about the heart – God values sincerity and humility in worship over outward expressions.

Generosity is a divine calling – Wealth should not make us arrogant; instead, it should be used to do good and help others.

Spiritual transparency matters – God sees everything, so we should approach Him with honesty and a pure heart.

CHAPTER SEVEN

NAKEDNESS AND THE DANGER OF SUPERFICIAL WORSHIP

The idea of nakedness reflects the need for genuine humility and transparency before God. It challenges us to strip away layers of superficiality and pretense in our worship. In Isaiah 29:13, NIV, God addresses the issue of outward ritual without true heart alignment, saying, *"These people come near to me with their mouth and honor me with their lips, but their hearts are far from me. Their worship of me is based on merely human rules they have been taught."* This verse warns against worship that is only performed on the surface, without true devotion or understanding. Superficial worship is easy; it involves following rules, attending services, and participating in rituals without the deeper engagement of the heart. But God desires more than just ritualistic actions He desires a genuine relationship.

The danger of superficial worship is that it can become about external performance rather than a transformation of the heart. Jesus, quoting Isaiah, highlights this in Matthew 15:8, NIV, *"These people honor me with their lips, but their hearts are far from me."* This reinforces the idea that worship is not simply about doing the right things, such as wearing the right clothes or attending the right services. If these actions are not accompanied by heartfelt devotion, they lose their meaning. Nakedness in worship, therefore, is not about removing external adornments but about shedding pride, hypocrisy, and insincerity. It calls for a transparent relationship with God where we present ourselves fully, with all our flaws and needs, without pretending to be more than we are.

Nakedness in the spiritual sense calls us to examine our motivations and intentions. Are we worshiping God because we truly desire to honor Him, or are we going through the motions? Jesus criticizes the Pharisees for their outward religiosity in Luke 18:10-14, telling the parable of the Pharisee and the tax collector. The Pharisee, dressed in the finest clothes and praying with eloquence, thought himself righteous because of his external actions. However, his heart was far from God. The tax collector, in contrast, approached God humbly, acknowledging his sin and need for mercy. Jesus concluded, *"For all those who exalt themselves will be humbled, and those who humble themselves will be exalted."* True worship is about a humble, open heart before God, stripped of pride and self-righteousness. It is in this spiritual nakedness that we find true intimacy with God.

The concept of nakedness challenges us to reflect on our own worship practices and question whether they are genuine. Are we worshipping to impress others, to fulfil obligations, or because we desire to honor God? God's call to nakedness in worship is not about external appearances but about sincerity and humility. As 1 Samuel 16:7, NIV, reminds us, *"The Lord does not look at the things people look at. People look at the outward appearance, but the Lord looks at the heart."* God sees through any façade we put up. He desires authenticity, where our hearts are fully aligned with His will.

Superficial worship is often rooted in pride and hypocrisy. We may feel the need to present ourselves as spiritually superior, hiding our flaws or struggles in order to appear more righteous. However, God calls us to lay down these masks. Proverbs 11:2, NIV says, *"When pride comes, then comes disgrace, but with humility comes wisdom."* True nakedness before God requires us to strip away the pride that prevents us from acknowledging our need for His grace. It is through humility that we are able to experience true worship, where we acknowledge that everything, we have come from Him, and we offer our whole selves in service to His will.

NAKEDNESS AS OPENNESS TO GOD'S TRANSFORMATIVE WORK

Nakedness, as a spiritual metaphor, signifies the surrender of pretenses and defenses before God, allowing Him to work in us and transform us. Isaiah 29:15, NIV, reminds us of the futility of hiding from God: *"Woe to those who go to great depths to hide their plans from the Lord, who do their work in darkness and think, 'Who sees us? Who will know?'"* This verse underscores the truth that God sees beyond our external facades and directly into our hearts. When we come to Him in spiritual nakedness, we acknowledge His sovereignty and invite His transformative work into our lives. How often do we rely on appearances or self-sufficiency, forgetting that God desires our authenticity?

This openness requires us to relinquish our pride and admit our weaknesses. As Paul states in 2 Corinthians 12:9, NIV, *"But he said to me, 'My grace is sufficient for you, for my power is made perfect in weakness.'"* Nakedness before God allows Him to perfect His strength in our frailty, replacing our imperfections with His grace. Christian author Richard Foster writes, *"The desperate need today is not for a greater number of intelligent people, or gifted people, but for deep people."* True transformation begins when we expose the depth of our being to God's refining presence. What areas of our lives are we hesitant to surrender to Him?

Nakedness also represents a willingness to let go of sin and distractions that impede our spiritual growth. Hebrews 12:1, NIV, exhorts us to *"throw off everything that hinders and the sin that so easily entangles."* By shedding these hindrances, we allow God to purify our hearts and align us with His will. Approaching God with such openness can be intimidating, yet it is the path to becoming the person He has called us to be. Have we considered the blessings that could flow from giving God full access to our lives?

Through nakedness, we experience the renewal of our minds and the transformation of our character. Romans 12:2, NIV, urges, *"Do not conform to the pattern of this world, but be transformed by the renewing of your mind."* Transformation requires openness to God's correction, guidance, and sanctification. It is in this state of vulnerability that God reshapes our desires, priorities, and actions to reflect His glory. Nakedness teaches us to depend on God's transformative power rather than our own efforts. What steps can we take to cultivate this openness?

For future generations, the lesson is clear: a life of authenticity and surrender to God leads to genuine transformation. Nakedness, as a posture of humility, demonstrates that true strength and purpose come from allowing God to work within us. In a world often focused on appearances and self-reliance, this truth calls us to embrace vulnerability as the starting point of spiritual growth. Are we willing to model this openness for others, showing that God's transformative power is available to all who trust Him?

NAKEDNESS AND WORSHIP IN SPIRIT AND TRUTH

Nakedness calls us to worship God in spirit and truth, prioritizing the sincerity of our hearts over external practices. Nakedness in the spiritual sense urges us to strip away the distractions, pride, and pretense that often accompany our worship. The essence of true worship is not about outward rituals or appearances but about the inner condition of the heart. In John 4:24, NIV, Jesus teaches, *"God is spirit, and His worshipers must worship in spirit and in truth."* This verse emphasizes that God, being a spiritual being, desires worship that transcends physical forms and rituals. Worshiping in spirit and truth means offering ourselves sincerely to God, unburdened by external distractions, and aligning our hearts with His will. Nakedness, as a metaphor, represents this spiritual posture, where we come before God with complete honesty, vulnerability, and openness, acknowledging our need for His grace.

Many religious practices, such as wearing specific clothing or performing particular rituals, are often seen as expressions of devotion. While these practices can be meaningful when they reflect the heart's desire to honor God, they can become empty if not accompanied by true faith and humility. In Isaiah 29:13, NIV, God critiques those who worship with mere external displays: *"These people come near to me with their mouth and honor me with their lips, but their hearts are far from me."* This passage reveals that God is not impressed by superficial worship; He desires authenticity. Physical acts of worship, such as wearing white garments or rejecting worldly adornments, are only meaningful when they stem from a genuine desire to honor God and align our lives with His will. True nakedness in worship means that our external actions reflect an inner reality of devotion, purity, and truth.

TRUE NAKEDNESS IN WORSHIP: SINCERITY, HUMILITY, AND COMMITMENT

True nakedness in worship represents a state of sincerity, humility, and commitment before God. It transcends physical exposure and instead reveals the essence of our inner selves laid bare before Him. In Psalm 51:17, David proclaims, *"The sacrifices of God are a broken spirit; a broken and contrite heart you, God, will not despise"* (NIV). This verse shows that God values authenticity and humility above external rituals. True worship is not only about appearing perfect or righteous but about coming to God honestly, admitting our need for Him, and seeking His transformative presence.

Sincerity in worship requires the removal of pretense. Are we genuinely worshiping God, or are we simply going through the motions? In John 4:23-24, Jesus says, *"Yet a time is coming and has now come when the true worshipers will worship the Father in the Spirit and in truth, for they are the kind of worshipers the Father seeks. God is spirit, and his worshipers must worship in the Spirit and in truth"* (NIV). Worship in truth requires transparency and vulnerability before God. It is an acknowledgement of our flaws and a genuine desire to grow closer to Him. By shedding our masks, we invite God to work in us authentically.

Humility is another vital aspect of nakedness in worship. When we come before God without pride or self-righteousness, we allow Him to mold and guide us. James 4:10 says, *"Humble yourselves before the Lord, and he will lift you up"* (NIV). Christian author A.W. Tozer once wrote, *"True worship that is pleasing to God creates within the human heart a spirit of humility and a desire to be obedient to all that Christ commands."* When we worship with humility, we submit to God's sovereignty, acknowledging that He alone is worthy of our praise and devotion.

Commitment in worship means offering our entire selves to God, holding nothing back. Romans 12:1 encourages believers to present themselves as *"a living sacrifice, holy and pleasing to God this is your true and proper worship"* (NIV). This level of dedication requires us to prioritize God above all else, aligning our actions, thoughts, and desires with His will. Nakedness in worship is a commitment to staying true to God even when it is inconvenient or costly, trusting that His plans are greater than our own.

For current and generations to come, the lesson of true nakedness in worship is profound. It teaches us to prioritize authenticity in our relationship with God over appearances or rituals. Are we willing to humble ourselves before God, admit our vulnerabilities, and commit to following Him wholeheartedly? In a world that often values outward success over inner transformation, the concept of true nakedness challenges us to focus on what truly matters our heart's posture toward God. This approach to worship not only deepens our faith but also serves as a testimony of God's transformative power to those around us.

WORSHIPING IN TRUTH: A COMMITMENT TO GOD'S WILL

Worshipping in truth is more than verbal expressions of praise; it is a deep commitment to aligning one's life with the will and Word of God. Jesus affirms this in John 14:6 (NKJV), stating, *"I am the way, the truth, and the life. No one comes to the Father except through Me."* Worship in truth acknowledges Christ as the embodiment of divine truth and seeks to conform every aspect of life to His teachings. True worship is not confined to church services or rituals; it is a way of living that reflects obedience to God's will and a heart committed to His glory.

True worship calls us to examine our motives and actions. Are we worshiping God with sincerity, or are we simply fulfilling an obligation? Jesus highlights this in John 4:23-24 (NKJV): *"But the hour is coming, and now is, when the true worshipers will worship the Father in spirit and truth; for the Father is seeking such to worship Him. God is Spirit, and those who worship Him must worship in spirit and truth."* Worship in truth requires authenticity, where we shed pretense and offer God our genuine devotion. It is a commitment to live out what we profess, reflecting God's truth in every decision, relationship, and endeavor.

Christian author A.W. Tozer observed, *"Worship acceptable to God is the overflow of a heart devoted to the Lord."* This means worship is not just an external act but an internal reality. Nakedness in this context symbolizes the vulnerability required to admit our flaws and submit to God's transformative work. How often do we approach God with hidden sins or divided loyalties, unwilling to fully surrender? Worshipping in truth demands a willingness to confront and remove these barriers, allowing God's Word to refine and guide us.

Commitment to God's will also means trusting His sovereignty, even when life's circumstances are challenging. Romans 12:1 (NKJV) exhorts believers to present their bodies as *"a living sacrifice, holy, acceptable to God, which is your reasonable service."* This act of worship involves dedicating every part of our lives to God's purposes. It reminds us that true worship is not just about what we say but what we do, how we serve, and how we love others. This alignment with God's will demonstrates a worshipful life that honors Him beyond the walls of a church building.

Therefore, the lesson here is clear: worshipping in truth requires sincerity, obedience, and a lifestyle that reflects God's will. In a world filled with distractions, falsehoods, and superficial commitments, this truth challenges believers to live with integrity and purpose. Are we willing to worship God not just with our lips but with our lives? By prioritizing truth and aligning with God's will, we leave a legacy of faithfulness that inspires others to seek a deeper, more authentic relationship with Him.

WORSHIPPING WITH A PURE HEART

Worshipping with a pure heart is central to a meaningful relationship with God. In Matthew 5:8 (NKJV), Jesus declares, *"Blessed are the pure in heart, for they shall see God."* This beatitude highlights the importance of purity in our approach to worship. A pure heart is one that is undivided and seeks God above all else, free from ulterior motives or distractions. Worshipping with a pure heart involves stripping away the layers of self-interest, pride, and hypocrisy, allowing God's truth to cleanse and renew us. It reflects a sincere desire to honor God for who He is, not for what we can gain from Him.

The essence of worship with a pure heart is sincerity and authenticity. In Psalm 51:10 (NKJV), David cries out, *"Create in me a clean heart, O God, and renew a steadfast spirit within me."* This heartfelt prayer acknowledges that purity is not something we achieve on our own; it is a work of God's grace. A pure heart is not about perfection but about humility and openness to God's transformative power. Are we willing to confront the hidden motives and sins that may hinder our worship? Are we prepared to let go of distractions and focus entirely on God's presence?

Christian author Andrew Murray once wrote, *"Humility is the only soil in which grace takes root."* Worshiping with a pure heart requires humility a willingness to acknowledge our dependence on God and admit our need for His cleansing. This humility allows us to approach God in spiritual nakedness, offering ourselves just as we are. By doing so, we create space for God to work within us, shaping our hearts to align with His will. Nakedness in worship symbolizes this openness, where we hide nothing from God and trust in His mercy to cover us.

Worship with a pure heart also reflects obedience to God's commands. In John 14:15 (NKJV), Jesus says, *"If you love Me, keep My commandments."* A pure heart is marked by a desire to honor God not just in worship but in every aspect of life. This purity extends beyond words and rituals to the way we live, love, and serve others. Are our lives consistent with the worship we offer to God? Worshiping with a pure heart calls us to align our actions with our faith, ensuring that our devotion is genuine and complete.

For current and future generations, worshiping with a pure heart serves as a timeless lesson in sincerity and humility. In an age where appearances often take precedence over authenticity, this call to purity reminds us of what truly matters: a heart devoted to God. Are we teaching the next generation to prioritize their relationship with God over the distractions of the world? By modeling and encouraging worship with a pure heart, we inspire others to seek God with sincerity, ensuring that worship remains a true reflection of faith and love for Him.

NAKEDNESS BEFORE GOD: AUTHENTIC WORSHIP FROM THE HEART

Nakedness before God, in a spiritual sense, represents the vulnerability and honesty required for genuine worship. Just as physical nakedness removes all barriers and pretensions, spiritual nakedness before God involves laying bare our hearts before Him. It means offering ourselves in truth, without trying to hide our flaws, sins, or imperfections. This level of transparency is essential for authentic worship that is not just a formality or an act of outward devotion, but a deep, sincere expression of love and submission to God's will.

Throughout Scripture, God consistently emphasizes that true worship arises from the heart, not merely from outward expressions. In Ezekiel 33:31, NIV, we encounter a sobering portrayal of people who hear God's word but fail to live by it: *"My people come to you, as they usually do, and sit before you to listen to your words, but they do not put them into practice. Their mouths speak of love, but their hearts are greedy for unjust gain."* This passage shows that while people may outwardly listen to God's word and even speak about His love, their actions betray their lack of true commitment. Their worship is superficial because it is not backed by sincere devotion or obedience. The essence of worship, therefore, is not in the ritual or the act of listening, but in the sincere application of God's Word in our lives.

Similarly, in Matthew 15:7-9, Jesus critiques the Pharisees and teachers of the law, condemning their hollow worship. He says, *"You hypocrites! Isaiah was right when he prophesied about you: 'These people honor me with their lips, but their hearts are far from me. They worship me in vain; their teachings are merely human rules."* Jesus points out that worship that is merely lip service—empty words without heartfelt commitment does not honor God. This highlights the difference between outward expressions of worship and the inward reality that must accompany them. Worship that honors God comes from a heart that is fully surrendered, one that is aligned with His will, and one that seeks to live according to His truth.

These passages remind us that God values authenticity over appearances. In our relationship with God, it is not enough to simply go through the motions of religious activity. What matters most is the sincerity behind those actions. God desires to be worshiped in spirit and in truth (John 4:24), not through rituals that are disconnected from our inner reality. Nakedness before God reflects this openness a willingness to be seen as we are, with all our flaws, sins, and desires, but with the intent to turn our hearts towards Him and submit to His will.

NOTE THESE

True worship comes from the heart – Worship should be sincere, not just an outward act or ritual.

Purity leads to closeness with God – A pure heart allows us to see and experience God more deeply.

Humility is essential in worship – Acknowledging our need for God's grace enables genuine devotion.

Obedience reflects true worship – Loving God means following His commandments, not just praising Him with words.

God values authenticity over appearance – He desires honesty and transparency rather than superficial acts of devotion.

CHAPTER EIGHT

NAKEDNESS AS OPENNESS AND SURRENDER

Spiritual nakedness symbolizes an unguarded and honest posture before God, where there is no attempt to conceal our flaws, fears, or failures. This openness reflects our willingness to expose every aspect of ourselves to Him. In Hebrews 4:13 (NKJV), it says, *"And there is no creature hidden from His sight, but all things are naked and open to the eyes of Him to whom we must give account."* This verse reminds us that we cannot hide from God, as He sees our hearts and knows our innermost thoughts. Nakedness in this sense is not something to fear but an opportunity to engage with God on the most profound level. By coming before Him without pretense, we demonstrate trust in His mercy and sovereignty.

True surrender requires vulnerability, and spiritual nakedness is a call to let go of the masks we often wear. It's about shedding pride, self-reliance, and pretense, allowing God to work in our lives. David's prayer in Psalm 139:23-24 (NKJV) illustrates this openness: *"Search me, O God, and know my heart; try me, and know my anxieties; and see if there is any wicked way in me, and lead me in the way everlasting."* This prayer reflects a deep trust in God's goodness, as David invites God to examine his life and guide him toward transformation. Are we willing to make ourselves this vulnerable before God?

This openness before God also facilitates spiritual renewal. Just as physical nakedness symbolizes vulnerability and purity, spiritual nakedness allows us to be cleansed and made whole by God's grace. Psalm 51:17 (NKJV) declares, *"The sacrifices of God are a broken spirit, a broken and contrite heart these, O God, You will not despise."* God desires humility and a repentant heart that acknowledges its need for His mercy. When we are open to God's transformative work, He replaces our shame with joy, our fear with confidence, and our sin with righteousness.

Christian author A.W. Tozer once said, *"We must hide nothing from God and confess everything with open, honest hearts. We must be willing to be humbled."* Nakedness as openness and surrender is a powerful act of humility, acknowledging that we cannot transform ourselves. Are we clinging to our own abilities, or are we surrendering to the One who can truly make us new? This question challenges us to reflect on the depth of our trust in God's power to heal and renew us.

For current and future generations, this concept underscores the importance of authenticity in our relationship with God. In a world that often prioritizes appearances and self-sufficiency, spiritual nakedness teaches us to value transparency, humility, and dependence on God. By modeling openness and surrender, we set an example for others to trust God fully, allowing Him to shape their lives for His glory. This timeless lesson encourages a deeper, more meaningful walk with God one that leads to lasting transformation and peace.

NAKEDNESS AND THE TRANSFORMATION OF THE HEART

Spiritual nakedness is an internal posture of vulnerability before God. It is an invitation for God to transform our hearts, removing pretense, pride, and hypocrisy, and replacing them with genuine devotion and obedience. This transformation begins with our willingness to be exposed before God, acknowledging our flaws and our need for His grace. Just as physical nakedness removes all coverings and facades, spiritual nakedness allows God to see our innermost thoughts and desires, enabling Him to mold us into His likeness. When we embrace spiritual nakedness, we surrender our hearts to His work, allowing His will to be reflected in every aspect of our lives.

In Ezekiel 33:3, NIV, the people of Israel offer empty expressions of devotion, but their actions betray their true hearts: *"My people come to you, as they usually do, and sit before you to listen to your words, but they do not put them into practice. Their mouths speak of love, but their hearts are greedy for unjust gain."* Despite the outward appearance of worship, their hearts are full of greed and disobedience. This highlights those outward expressions of worship or devotion become hollow if they are not backed by true inner transformation. Nakedness before God, therefore, is not just about what is seen on the outside, but about inviting God into the innermost parts of our lives to purify and transform us.

Similarly, in Matthew 15:7-9, NIV, Jesus rebukes the Pharisees and teachers of the law, pointing out their hypocrisy: *"You hypocrites! Isaiah was right when he prophesied about you: 'These people honor me with their lips, but their hearts are far from me. They worship me in vain; their teachings are merely human rules.'"* Here, Jesus exposes the discrepancy between their outward worship and their inner condition. While they followed rituals and recited the right words, their hearts were far from God. This emphasizes that true worship and transformation occur not in ritualistic acts alone but in the alignment of our hearts with God's will. Nakedness, in this sense, represents the stripping away of all pretensions and facades, allowing God to cleanse us from the inside out.

Consider an individual who hears a sermon on forgiveness but continues to harbor resentment and unforgiveness toward someone who has wronged them. On the surface, they may attend church, participate in worship, and even express a desire to live according to God's Word. However, their unwillingness to forgive undermines the transformative power of the gospel in their lives. Despite hearing God's word, their failure to apply it reveals a heart that is not fully surrendered to God's will.

When such an individual embraces spiritual nakedness, they open their hearts to God's transforming work. This means acknowledging their bitterness and asking God for the strength to forgive. As they surrender their resentment to God, they begin to align their actions with His teachings, demonstrating the authenticity of their faith. In doing so, their worship becomes genuine, and their lives reflect the transformative power of God's Word. This process of transformation is central to spiritual nakedness. It's not just about outward appearances but about allowing God to change our hearts and guide our actions.

NAKEDNESS AS A CALL TO ALIGN FAITH AND ACTION

True nakedness before God bridges the gap between hearing His word and living it, challenging us to align our faith with our actions. Nakedness before God is not merely about an outward appearance but about a deep, internal transformation that calls for integrity and genuine devotion. It requires more than passive belief; it calls for active obedience. True nakedness before God involves laying aside all pretense and submitting to His will, both in our hearts and in our actions. When we embrace this spiritual nakedness, we acknowledge that faith is not a passive feeling but a dynamic force that compels us to live according to God's Word. It changes our behavior, guiding us to reflect God's teachings in every part of our lives.

James 1:22, NIV emphasizes the importance of aligning our actions with what we hear from God: *"Do not merely listen to the word, and so deceive yourselves. Do what it says."* This verse challenges us to avoid the trap of hearing God's Word without allowing it to shape our lives. In a world where many people claim to follow God but fail to live according to His commands, this call to action is essential. Just as nakedness removes all coverings, we must remove the barriers of hypocrisy, selfishness, and indifference that prevent us from living out God's Word.

Nakedness, in this spiritual sense, symbolizes the stripping away of all external facades and pretenses. It is not enough to wear the *"garment"* of devotion without allowing the change to permeate our hearts and actions. Nakedness before God demands integrity and obedience. It is a state of being where our inner faith aligns seamlessly with what we express outwardly. This kind of transparency in our relationship with God leads to a transformation where our actions reflect His will and His truth. When we choose to live in this way, we become living testimonies of God's power and grace. Our faith is no longer a mere intellectual assent but becomes a lived reality. Every action, every word, and every decision should be an extension of our faith, demonstrating that we are truly living out the principles that God has spoken into our lives.

NAKEDNESS AND SELF-REFLECTION

Nakedness invites us to examine our motivations, challenging us to identify areas where our actions fall short of God's standards. Nakedness before God is not only a physical concept but also a deep spiritual invitation to self-examination. It encourages us to reflect on our hearts, intentions, and motivations in light of God's holiness and truth. Just as being physically naked removes all external coverings, spiritual nakedness requires us to strip away the layers of pride, self-deception, and worldly influence that distort our relationship with God. This vulnerable self-reflection leads to greater alignment with His will, as we honestly evaluate our lives and identify areas where we need His transformation.

The practice of self-reflection in the context of nakedness before God challenges us to examine whether our actions align with His standards or if they are motivated by personal desires, external pressures, or social expectations. A key example of this can be seen in the way consumer behavior is often influenced by advertising and societal trends. Consumers are encouraged to prioritize certain products, lifestyles, or appearances based on external messaging rather than their true needs or values. This external influence can easily shape our priorities, causing us to make decisions that reflect societal norms rather than God's will.

Also, in a spiritual context, nakedness before God invites us to reflect on whether our motivations are shaped by the expectations of others or by our own self-interest, rather than being driven by a sincere desire to honor God. This kind of nakedness means allowing the Holy Spirit to illuminate the areas of our lives where we have been influenced by the world, where our worship has become mechanical, or where we've allowed pride or selfishness to obscure our true devotion to God. It calls us to examine whether our actions, whether in worship, service, or daily life, are truly reflective of God's Word or whether they are motivated by personal gain or external validation.

The concept of nakedness as self-reflection is beautifully illustrated in Psalm 139:23-24, NIV, where David prays: *"Search me, O God, and know my heart; test me and know my anxious thoughts. See if there is any offensive way in me, and lead me in the way everlasting."* This prayer is a powerful example of spiritual nakedness—David is inviting God to examine his innermost thoughts and motivations, allowing God to reveal any areas where his actions do not align with His will.

Additionally, in Hebrews 4:12, NIV, it says: *"For the word of God is alive and active. Sharper than any double-edged sword, it penetrates even to dividing soul and spirit, joints and marrow; it judges the thoughts and attitudes of the heart."* This verse shows the role of God's Word in helping us engage in deep self-reflection. The Bible serves as a mirror, revealing the truth about our hearts and actions, and guiding us toward spiritual maturity.

LIVING IN SPIRITUAL NAKEDNESS

Nakedness before God is a call to authenticity, obedience, and transformation. It demands that we align our hearts with His will, allowing His word to shape our actions. Spiritual nakedness goes beyond the symbolic act of stripping away external layers; it calls us to strip away all pretense, self-reliance, and insincerity in our relationship with God. To live in spiritual nakedness is to approach God without the coverings of pride, self-justification, or superficial displays of worship. It is to embrace total vulnerability before God, acknowledging our dependence on Him and our need for His transforming grace. In this state of spiritual nakedness, we are called to live in authenticity, where our actions align with the desires of our hearts, and our hearts reflect God's will.

Nakedness before God requires authenticity an honest, open relationship with Him where there are no hidden motives or outward facades. This is not simply about outward religious expressions but about the condition of the heart. Ezekiel 33:31, NIV, describes a people who hear God's word but fail to put it into practice, saying, *"They come to you as people come, and they sit before you as my people. They hear your words, but they do not put them into practice."* This passage highlights how superficial worship, where external actions do not align with inner beliefs, grieves God. Worship that is not heartfelt is akin to a lie, offering lip service rather than genuine devotion.

Jesus also critiques this kind of false worship in Matthew 15:7-9, NIV, where He says, *"You hypocrites! Isaiah was right when he prophesied about you: 'These people honor me with their lips, but their hearts are far from me. They worship me in vain; their teachings are merely human rules."* This warning speaks to the danger of living a life of external religiosity that lacks inner transformation. It is a call to examine whether our worship, service, and faith reflect the sincerity of our hearts or are merely external practices without true devotion to God.

SPIRITUAL TRANSFORMATION

True spiritual nakedness involves a deep willingness to undergo transformation that begins at the heart and radiates outward. It is not merely about outwardly conforming to religious expectations but about allowing God to work within us, reshaping our character and desires. In Ezekiel 36:26 (NKJV), God promises, *"I will give you a new heart and put a new spirit within you; I will take the heart of stone out of your flesh and give you a heart of flesh."* This divine promise illustrates the essence of spiritual transformation it is God's work in us, requiring our surrender and openness to His refining process.

Spiritual transformation demands obedience and alignment with God's will. As Jesus emphasized in John 14:15 (NKJV), *"If you love Me, keep My commandments."* Genuine love for God translates into actions that honor Him. This obedience flows naturally from a heart that has been transformed, not as a duty but as a joyful response to His grace. Are we willing to let God shape us, even when it challenges our comfort or preferences? This question invites self-reflection on whether we prioritize God's will over our own desires.

Apostle Paul captures the continuous nature of spiritual transformation in Romans 12:2 (NKJV), urging believers to *"be transformed by the renewing of your mind."* Transformation is not a one-time event but a daily process of choosing God's truth over worldly patterns. This renewal requires intentional engagement with Scripture, prayer, and community. As Christian author Dallas Willard said, *"The most important thing in your life is not what you do; it's who you become."* Transformation involves becoming more like Christ, and this process requires us to consistently open ourselves to God's guidance.

Spiritual nakedness calls us to authenticity. It strips away pretense and hypocrisy, encouraging us to live in a way that reflects the inward change God has worked in us. Matthew 23:26 (NKJV) warns against outward appearances that do not align with inward purity: *"First cleanse the inside of the cup and dish, that the outside of them may be clean also."* Are we living authentically, or are we more concerned with appearances? This challenge compels us to examine whether our faith is genuine and impactful.

So, the lesson of spiritual transformation demonstrate the importance of authenticity and growth in faith. It teaches that true change begins within, shaping how we live and interact with others. Therefore, modeling a transformed life, we demonstrate the power of God's grace and the beauty of a surrendered heart. This testimony encourages others to seek a deeper relationship with God, knowing that His transformative work leads to eternal joy and peace.

COMMITMENT TO INTEGRITY

Living authentically in spiritual nakedness requires an unwavering commitment to integrity. Integrity means aligning our actions with our words and ensuring that our lives reflect the truths we profess. Jesus highlights this principle in Matthew 5:37 (NKJV): *"But let your 'Yes' be 'Yes,' and your 'No,' 'No.' For whatever is more than these is from the evil one."* This teaching calls for honesty, simplicity, and consistency, both in our dealings with others and in our relationship with God. Integrity is the foundation of a faith-filled life, as it demonstrates our trust in God and our desire to honor Him in all things.

Consider the dangers of hypocrisy, where outward appearances do not align with inward realities. As Jesus rebuked the Pharisees in Matthew 23:28 (NKJV): *"Even so you also outwardly appear righteous to men, but inside you are full of hypocrisy and lawlessness."* Is it possible to genuinely serve God while living a double life? This challenges us to examine our hearts and actions, ensuring that they are consistent with the values of God's kingdom. Integrity in spiritual nakedness involves confessing our shortcomings and seeking God's help to live authentically, without masks or pretense.

A commitment to integrity also means standing firm in truth, even when it is inconvenient or countercultural. Proverbs 10:9 (NKJV) reminds us, *"He who walks with integrity walks securely, but he who perverts his ways will become known."* Walking in integrity brings peace and confidence, as we have nothing to hide. On the other hand, deceit and dishonesty ultimately lead to exposure and shame. Christian author Charles Spurgeon once said, *"A lie can travel halfway around the world while the truth is putting on its shoes, but truth walks steadily, and its victory is certain."* This calls us to be steadfast in our commitment to truth, trusting that integrity will ultimately prevail.

Integrity demands that we live with transparency before God and others. Spiritual nakedness compels us to open our hearts fully to God, acknowledging both our strengths and weaknesses. Psalm 139:23-24 (NKJV) says, *"Search me, O God, and know my heart; try me, and know my anxieties; and see if there is any wicked way in me, and lead me in the way everlasting."* This willingness to invite God's scrutiny reflects a heart that values integrity over appearances. Are we willing to let God examine our motives and transform us into people of genuine character?

For both current and future generations, a life of integrity is a powerful testimony of faith. It reminds us that true worship is not confined to rituals but is demonstrated through our daily choices and actions. As we live with authenticity, we inspire others to pursue a life of honesty, humility, and faithfulness. Integrity honors God and reflects His nature, leaving a legacy of trustworthiness and faith for those who follow. Ultimately, it challenges all believers to align their lives with God's will, knowing that He sees and rewards those who walk in truth.

NAKEDNESS AS A SYMBOL OF FREEDOM FROM SOCIETAL PRESSURES

In the biblical account of Adam and Eve in Genesis 2:25, we see that they were *"both naked, and were not ashamed."* This state of nakedness symbolizes freedom, authenticity, and a life without the burden of societal expectations. They lived in complete harmony with God, free from the pressures and temptations that would later arise due to sin. Nakedness, in its truest sense, is a reflection of being unencumbered by the false expectations of the world and living fully in God's design for us. The freedom that Adam and Eve enjoyed before the fall is the type of freedom God calls us to reclaim spiritually free from the shackles of societal pressures that attempt to shape us according to worldly standards.

In today's world, we are constantly bombarded with societal norms, consumer trends, and cultural expectations that shape how we think, live, and make decisions. Whether it's the pursuit of material wealth, keeping up with the latest fashion trends, or conforming to the ideals of beauty and success, the pressure to fit into society's mold can often outweigh our desire to follow God's principles. As the example of consumer behavior illustrates, societal trends often create a cycle of inadequacy and conformity, where people feel the need to buy things, act in certain ways, or appear a certain way in order to be accepted or validated. This pursuit of outward success and approval can lead to a sense of emptiness, as the core of our identity remains rooted in external factors rather than in who we are in Christ.

The Bible addresses this very issue in Ezekiel 33:31, NIV, where God condemns the people for listening to His word but not living it out: *"They come to you as people come, and they sit before you as my people. They hear your words, but they do not put them into practice."* This behavior reflects the way many today is shaped by societal norms and trends, listening to God's word but prioritizing the outward appearances and practices that society values over genuine transformation. Similarly, in Matthew 15:7-9, NIV, Jesus critiques the Pharisees for honoring God with their lips while their hearts were far from Him, emphasizing that external religious practices without sincere devotion are ultimately empty: *"You hypocrites! Isaiah was right when he prophesied about you: 'These people honor me with their lips, but their hearts are far from me.'"*

In the same way that Adam and Eve were originally free from external pressures, spiritual nakedness challenges us to remove the layers of pretense, materialism, and external validation that cloud our relationship with God. It calls us to break free from these worldly influences and focus on cultivating a heart of genuine devotion to God, where our actions and beliefs align with His will, not societal expectations.

Consider a person in today's society who feels constant pressure to fit into the latest trends in fashion, technology, or social behavior. They might spend beyond their means to keep up with what's "in," constantly feeling inadequate when they don't have the latest gadgets or the "right" clothes. Spiritually, this pressure to conform to external standards is reflected in a tendency to prioritize outward religious practices attending church, reciting prayers, or following rituals—without allowing those actions to flow from a genuine heart of faith and devotion. This can lead to spiritual disillusionment and a sense of emptiness, as the deeper connection with God is lost in the pursuit of societal approval.

Similarly, in the church, some individuals may feel the need to conform to particular religious norms, such as the way they dress or speak, to appear more spiritual or pious. However, these outward practices, if disconnected from the heart, do not reflect true worship. The challenge of spiritual nakedness is to reject such external pressures and to focus on the authentic relationship with God that transcends these worldly expectations.

NAKEDNESS AS VULNERABILITY AND HUMILITY

God's choice to leave Adam and Eve in their original state of nakedness emphasizes the importance of vulnerability and humility, teaching reliance on Him rather than human traditions or societal norms. In the creation narrative, God chose to create Adam and Eve in a state of nakedness, which initially symbolized their purity, innocence, and complete reliance on Him. Genesis 2:25, NIV notes, *"And they were both naked, the man and his wife, and were not ashamed."* This nakedness was not merely physical but also spiritual. They were vulnerable and unprotected, dependent solely on God for everything. This state of being was a reflection of how humans were created to live in total humility, without reliance on anything other than their Creator. It is significant that God did not adorn them with any materialistic covering or decoration, underscoring that their identity and security were to be found in their relationship with Him, not in external appearances or societal expectations.

Nakedness, in its deepest spiritual sense, strips away all pretense and false securities. It exposes individuals for who they truly are vulnerable, dependent, and in need of divine provision. Just as Adam and Eve were exposed before God without shame, we too are called to live in spiritual nakedness free of pride, ego, and the need for self-reliance.

This is a position of vulnerability, where we can no longer hide behind our achievements, status, or material wealth, but are fully open before God, acknowledging that everything we have and is a gift from Him.

This sense of vulnerability is very key in our relationship with God. In Matthew 15:7-9, NIV, Jesus rebukes the Pharisees for their superficial worship, which was rooted in external traditions rather than an honest, humble heart. *"You hypocrites! Isaiah was right when he prophesied about you: 'These people honor me with their lips, but their hearts are far from me. They worship me in vain; their teachings are merely human rules."* Jesus emphasizes that worship is not about external compliance with rituals or traditions, but about the sincerity and humility of the heart. Nakedness before God, therefore, is not just a physical act but a spiritual one, where we strip away all the layers of self-deception, pride, and human expectation to stand before God in complete humility.

Nakedness calls us to recognize our dependence on God, acknowledging that we are nothing without His grace and mercy. It is a declaration that we do not need to rely on human traditions, external approval, or societal standards to define who we are or how we should live. True humility before God means accepting our vulnerability and surrendering our will to Him, trusting that He knows what is best for us.

NAKEDNESS AS A CALL TO AUTHENTIC WORSHIP

Nakedness invites us to worship God in spirit and truth, rejecting superficial expressions of faith influenced by societal expectations. Nakedness in a spiritual sense calls us to a place of authenticity and sincerity in our worship of God. It challenges us to discard all the facades we often build in our lives whether through societal pressures, external expectations, or self-imposed roles. In its most insightful form, spiritual nakedness is about standing before God with no pretense, no hiding, and no distractions, allowing our true selves to be fully exposed and vulnerable in His presence. This is the essence of authentic worship that goes beyond external actions and touches the very core of our hearts and lives.

In Isaiah 29:13, NIV, God warns against superficial worship that is not grounded in the heart: *"The Lord says: 'These people come near to me with their mouth and honor me with their lips, but their hearts are far from me. Their worship of me is based on merely human rules they have been taught."* This verse highlights the danger of honoring God outwardly while the heart remains distant. The Israelites were going through the motions of worship—offering sacrifices, praying, and following rituals but their hearts were far from God. Their worship was not genuine, but rather a hollow act designed to meet external expectations.

Similarly, in Matthew 15:8-9, NIV, Jesus critiques the Pharisees for their external show of religiosity: *"These people honor me with their lips, but their hearts are far from me. They worship me in vain; their teachings are merely human rules."* Here, Jesus condemns those who were concerned with ritual and tradition but lacked true devotion to God. Their faith had become mechanical, focused on outward appearance rather than an inner transformation. Jesus makes it clear that worship is not about external gestures but about the alignment of the heart with God's will.

NAKEDNESS: A RETURN TO AUTHENTICITY

It is a call to reject the external pressures and human traditions that often shape our faith and worship. Just as Adam and Eve were naked before God in their innocence, unashamed and unadorned by anything other than their natural state, we too are called to approach God in a state of spiritual nakedness open, vulnerable, and honest. Our worship, like our relationship with God, should not be an act we perform to please others or to conform to societal norms, but should spring from a deep, genuine love and reverence for God.

True worship is about aligning our hearts with God's will. It means removing the masks we wear and allowing ourselves to be seen as we truly are sinful, broken, and dependent on God for grace and mercy. This is the essence of worshiping in spirit and truth, as Jesus describes in John 4:24: *"God is spirit, and His worshipers must worship in the Spirit and in truth."* Worship that is in spirit and truth acknowledges our vulnerability before God, recognizing that we are nothing without Him.

NOTE THESE

Vulnerability before God fosters humility – True worship requires openness and dependence on Him.

Authenticity matters more than outward rituals – God desires sincere devotion, not just religious traditions.

Spiritual nakedness removes pride and self-reliance – True faith acknowledges our need for God's grace.

Worship should align with the heart, not just words – External acts are meaningless without genuine inner commitment.

True identity and security come from God – Relying on human approval or societal norms hinders authentic faith.

CHAPTER NINE

NAKEDNESS AS FREEDOM IN GOD'S TRUTH

Nakedness teaches us to embrace God's truth over human traditions, offering freedom from the ever-changing demands of society. Nakedness in the spiritual sense represents liberation freedom from the weight of societal expectations and the human traditions that often obscure God's eternal truths. It calls believers to a life of authenticity, one that prioritizes God's unchanging word over the fleeting and often conflicting norms of the world. By embracing spiritual nakedness, Christians are encouraged to align themselves with God's principles, finding true freedom in His truth.

Society often dictates standards of success, worth, and identity, pressuring individuals to conform to its ever-changing demands. These pressures can cause a disconnect between the values society promotes and the eternal truths God reveals in Scripture. Jesus addresses this tension in Matthew 15:9, NIV, when He says, *"They worship me in vain; their teachings are merely human rules."* This passage critiques those who prioritize human traditions over God's word, reducing worship to an act devoid of sincerity and divine alignment.

Spiritual nakedness invites believers to reject such influences and instead fully embrace God's truth. It represents a state of humility and reliance on God, where individuals strip away pretenses, pride, and the desire to conform to worldly standards. John 8:31-32, NIV, further emphasizes the liberating power of God's truth: *"If you hold to my teaching, you are really my disciples. Then you will know the truth, and the truth will set you free."* This freedom is not merely from sin but also from the anxieties and constraints imposed by societal norms.

Moreover, societal values often encourage behaviors and priorities that conflict with God's design, such as idolizing material wealth or pursuing recognition at the expense of integrity. Paul warns against this in Romans 12:2: *"Do not conform to the pattern of this world, but be transformed by the renewing of your mind."* Nakedness symbolizes this transformation, where believers shed the false securities provided by the world and choose to live in alignment with God's eternal truth.

Consider an individual who feels immense pressure to succeed in their career, believing their worth is defined by their achievements and possessions. This pursuit of material success might lead them to neglect their faith, family, and personal well-being. However, by embracing spiritual nakedness, they reject this societal expectation and instead focus on living according to God's truth. They come to understand that their worth is not determined by worldly accomplishments but by their identity as a child of God.

This perspective offers freedom and peace, enabling the individual to live with purpose and integrity. They find joy not in societal approval but in fulfilling God's calling, whether through acts of kindness, fostering relationships, or dedicating time to spiritual growth. Their life becomes a testimony to the truth of Matthew 6:33: *"But seek first His kingdom and His righteousness, and all these things will be given to you as well."*

COMPLETE SURRENDER: THE HEART OF TRUE DEVOTION

Complete surrender to God symbolizes the vulnerability and openness that He desires in our relationship with Him. Spiritual nakedness is a metaphor for laying aside pretense, pride, and superficiality, allowing our hearts to be fully exposed before God. This surrender reflects profound humility and trust in God's sovereignty, acknowledging that we cannot lead ourselves. Proverbs 23:26 (NKJV) states, *"My son, give me your heart, and let your eyes observe my ways."* This plea from God reveals His desire for our complete devotion and unfiltered commitment, not outward displays of religiosity.

True surrender means offering God our innermost selves our strengths, weaknesses, and hidden struggles. In John 4:23-24 (NKJV), Jesus teaches, *"The hour is coming, and now is, when the true worshipers will worship the Father in spirit and truth; for the Father is seeking such to worship Him. God is Spirit, and those who worship Him must worship in spirit and truth."* Spiritual nakedness represents this authentic worship, where nothing is hidden from God, and the worshiper fully acknowledges their dependence on Him. How often do we approach God with transparency, free from the masks we wear in daily life?

Living in complete surrender also involves releasing the attachments and ambitions that hinder our walk with God. Jesus underscores this principle in Matthew 16:24-25 (NKJV): *"If anyone desires to come after Me, let him deny himself, and take up his cross, and follow Me. For whoever desires to save his life will lose it, but whoever loses his life for My sake will find it."* This call to self-denial and faith is a cornerstone of spiritual surrender. Are we willing to strip away the comforts and distractions that keep us from fully embracing God's will?

Christian author Andrew Murray beautifully states, "God is ready to assume full responsibility for the life wholly yielded to Him." This quote reminds us that surrendering to God does not leave us empty-handed; rather, it places our lives in the hands of the One who can lead us to our greatest purpose. Just as nakedness signifies vulnerability, it also reflects trust. When we surrender to God, we trust Him to provide, guide, and transform us into His likeness.

For current and future generations, complete surrender to God is a timeless lesson in humility and dependence. It teaches us that true fulfilment is found not in our achievements or possessions but in a heart fully devoted to God. Nakedness before Him challenges us to live authentically, seeking His kingdom above all else. By modeling lives of surrender, we can inspire others to pursue God wholeheartedly, creating a legacy of faith and devotion that glorifies Him.

WORSHIPING IN SPIRIT AND TRUTH: A CALL FOR GENUINE DEVOTION

True nakedness before God demands that worship be genuine, sincere, and deeply rooted in truth. It is not enough to go through the motions of religious practices without truly engaging with the God we worship. In spiritual terms, nakedness signifies a complete stripping away of the outer layers the superficial practices and external displays that often characterize worship. It is a call for authenticity, where worship goes beyond rituals and traditions to become a personal and intimate expression of the heart. Imagine a person standing before God without any pretense, exposing their true selves, not for the sake of appearance but because they desire to connect with God on a deeper, more intimate level. This is the essence of worship in spirit and truth.

In John 4:23-24, Jesus tells the Samaritan woman, *"Yet a time is coming and has now come when the true worshipers will worship the Father in spirit and truth, for they are the kind of worshipers the Father seeks. God is spirit, and his worshipers must worship in the spirit and in truth"* (NKJV). This statement from Jesus moves the focus away from the physical location or traditional practices of worship and onto the heart of the worshiper. True worship is not about where we are or what we do externally, but it's about worshiping from the depths of our hearts, where our spirit aligns with God's truth. Are we, as believers, worshiping in a way that reflects an authentic connection with God, or are we simply going through the motions because it's expected of us?

In the Old Testament, worship involved strict adherence to the Law, with rituals such as animal sacrifices and ceremonial cleansings. These practices were outward signs of devotion, and while they served a purpose, they were never meant to replace genuine heart devotion. However, with the coming of Jesus, a new covenant was established that emphasized the importance of inward transformation. Jesus, in Matthew 15:8-9 (NKJV), critiques those who rely on external forms of worship without sincere devotion: *"These people honor me with their lips, but their hearts are far from me. They worship me in vain; their teachings are merely human rules."* Jesus challenges us to examine whether our worship is genuinely rooted in love for God, or if it has become a mere ritualistic act. How often do we find ourselves worshiping without the heart truly being engaged?

True nakedness before God requires believers to move beyond the comfort of familiar traditions and rituals. It demands an honest self-reflection, asking whether our worship is influenced by societal norms, personal comfort, or mere tradition. Are we more concerned with the way others perceive our worship, or are we focused on aligning ourselves with God's truth and letting His Spirit move in us? It calls for a willingness to shed the layers of false devotion, allowing God to see our hearts and respond to our authentic desires for Him. When we remove the distractions of conformity and tradition, we invite God to renew our hearts and establish a more intimate relationship with Him.

In his book *True Worshipers*, Bob Kauflin writes, *"True worship is a response to the greatness of God and should be a natural outpouring of a heart that has been touched by His mercy and grace."* This quote underscores the idea that worship should not be about performing for others or following traditions mindlessly. It should be a heartfelt response to the love and grace we have received from God. As we embrace nakedness in worship stripping away external influences and false motives we offer ourselves fully to God, not just in ritual but in sincere devotion. This act of worship in spirit and truth serves as a lesson to current and future generations: that authentic worship transcends cultural expectations and is rooted in the genuine love and reverence we have for our Creator.

NAKEDNESS AS SELF-EXAMINATION: THE CALL TO AUTHENTIC FAITH

Spiritual nakedness is a call for self-examination, encouraging believers to look deeply into their hearts and lives to ensure that their worship and faith are genuine and not influenced by superficial motives. Just as a mirror reflects the true state of a person's appearance, spiritual nakedness reflects the inner condition of a believer's heart. It requires introspection, where one actively seeks to align actions with faith, ensuring that worship is not a performance but a reflection of authentic devotion. Picture a person standing before a mirror, fully exposed, not to admire their appearance, but to examine their true self. In the same way, nakedness before God invites believers to confront the hidden motives and thoughts that may hinder their relationship with Him.

Under the old covenant, worship often revolved around following external laws and rituals, a system enforced by religious authorities. These outward acts of devotion were markers of faithfulness, but they did not always reflect the true condition of the heart. When Jesus came, He shifted the focus to personal accountability and the internal transformation that would come through grace. The Apostle Paul reminds believers in 2 Corinthians 13:5 (NKJV), *"Examine yourselves to see whether you are in the faith; test yourselves."* This call to self-examine is crucial for ensuring that one's faith remains vibrant and free from hypocrisy. Are we merely going through the motions of faith, or are we truly living out the grace and truth that Christ offers?

In Matthew 7:16, (NKJV), Jesus says, *"By their fruit you will recognize them."* The fruit of a believer's life character traits like love, joy, peace, patience, and kindness—serve as evidence of a genuine and transformed heart. Nakedness, in this context, invites believers to confront the inconsistencies between their faith and their actions. It calls for vulnerability and openness, allowing God to reveal areas of their lives that may not yet reflect His character. How can we truly say we love God if our actions do not align with His commands? Are we willing to allow God to expose areas of sin or weakness in our hearts, or do we prefer to hide them behind a mask of outward religiosity?

Superficial worship, while seemingly pious, can be a deception. In Matthew 15:8 (NKJV), Jesus criticizes the religious leaders who *"honor me with their lips, but their hearts are far from me."* Their worship was external, but it lacked the genuine connection with God that comes from the heart. Spiritual nakedness challenges believers to strip away the facade of religious performance and be transparent before God. Are we willing to let go of pretense and invite God to search our hearts, no matter what He might reveal? True worship cannot be based on external appearances; it must be rooted in a deep and authentic relationship with God.

As believers engage in self-examination, they must also recognize that this process is ongoing and essential for spiritual growth. In The Pursuit of Holiness, Jerry Bridges writes, *"The pursuit of holiness is a lifelong endeavor, and one of the ways God helps us grow is by shining His light on the dark areas of our hearts."* Self-examination is not about condemning ourselves but about being open to God's work of sanctification. Nakedness before God is not a one-time event but a continual process of allowing Him to refine and transform us. This self-examination serves as a lesson for both current and future generations, reminding them that genuine faith requires introspection, authenticity, and a willingness to surrender to God's transformative work.

NAKEDNESS: VULNERABILITY AND ACCOUNTABILITY IN THE CHRISTIAN FAITH

Spiritual nakedness embodies the essence of vulnerability before God, where believers are called to lay aside all pretenses and self-deception, approaching God with a heart that is fully open and accountable. This form of nakedness is not about physical exposure, but rather an openness of heart that allows believers to stand before God without hiding their flaws, fears, or failures. It's an invitation to embrace the vulnerability that comes from recognizing one's dependence on God for grace and transformation. Just as a person who is exposed physically cannot hide behind clothing, spiritual nakedness requires believers to remove the protective barriers they may have built up around their hearts. Are we willing to be completely honest with God, even when it means facing our imperfections and inadequacies?

In the Old Testament, God gave laws and rituals to guide His people, and these were often enforced by priests and community leaders. The laws provided external structures of obedience, and individuals were accountable to those in authority. However, in the New Testament, with Christ's fulfilment of the law, there is a shift toward personal responsibility. Believers are no longer merely accountable to external authorities, but they are personally responsible for their own relationship with God and their spiritual growth. Galatians 6:4 (NKJV) states, *"But let each one examine his own work, and then he will have rejoicing in himself alone, and not in another."* This personal accountability is not just about individual action; it is about examining one's heart before God and taking responsibility for one's spiritual journey.

Spiritual nakedness before God calls believers to come as they are, without the barriers of pride, fear, or societal expectations. It is an acknowledgement of one's weaknesses, an understanding that no human strength or righteousness can substitute for God's grace. The call to vulnerability in worship is a powerful reminder that we cannot hide from God; He sees beyond the surface to the deepest parts of our hearts. As C.S. Lewis writes, *"We must lay before Him what is in us, not what ought to be in us."* Spiritual nakedness is the act of surrendering self-sufficiency and embracing God's transformative work in one's life. Do we have the courage to surrender everything, acknowledging that our growth is not based on our own strength but on God's grace and mercy?

The parable of the Pharisee and the tax collector in Luke 18:9-14 offers a vivid illustration of vulnerability and accountability before God. In the parable, the Pharisee is focused on his external righteousness, boasting about his piety and religious deeds. Meanwhile, the tax collector, deeply aware of his sinfulness, simply prays, *"God, be merciful to me, a sinner!"* (Luke 18:13 NKJV). Jesus praises the tax collector for his humility and vulnerability, teaching that true righteousness comes from an honest heart, not from external displays of piety. The Pharisee's pride represents the illusion of self-sufficiency, whereas the tax collector's vulnerability reveals the heart that God desires one that is open, humble, and willing to be accountable to Him.

Therefore, this concept of vulnerability and accountability has profound implications for both personal faith and the larger Christian community. In the body of Christ, vulnerability allows for genuine relationships that are not based on superficial appearances or external actions, but on authentic spiritual growth. As Paul writes in Galatians 6:5, *"For each one shall bear his own load."* This means that while we are part of a community, each believer is responsible for their own walk with God. Nakedness before God invites us to strip away the layers of pride and self-reliance, to stand before God with an honest heart, and to rely on His grace. Will we continue to walk in our own strength, or will we embrace the vulnerability that comes with acknowledging our need for God's mercy? This lesson serves as a reminder to both current and future generations that authentic faith begins with vulnerability before God and personal accountability in our spiritual journey.

NOTE THESE

Self-examination is essential for authentic faith – True worship requires deep introspection and honesty before God.

Faith must be lived out, not just professed – Genuine belief is reflected in actions, not just words.

Spiritual nakedness removes hypocrisy – God desires sincerity, not outward displays of religiosity.

Vulnerability before God leads to transformation – Surrendering pride and self-reliance allows God to refine our hearts.

Personal accountability is key to spiritual growth – Each believer is responsible for their own relationship with God.

CHAPTER TEN

THE BEAUTY OF SPIRITUAL OPENNESS BEFORE GOD

Spiritual openness before God is the act of laying bare our hearts, minds, and souls in His presence, allowing Him to see us as we truly are. This openness is not about exposing ourselves out of shame but out of a desire to experience God's redemptive love and grace. When we come to God with openness, we are acknowledging that we cannot hide from Him, and that He already knows our innermost thoughts, struggles, and desires. As Psalm 139:1-2 (NIV) says, *"You have searched me, Lord, and you know me. You know when I sit and when I rise; you perceive my thoughts from afar."* This verse highlights that there is no part of our lives hidden from God, yet He still desires us to come to Him openly and honestly.

The beauty of spiritual openness lies in the freedom it brings. When we stop pretending or hiding our flaws, we make space for true healing and growth. Being open before God means we are willing to be vulnerable and transparent, trusting that He will not condemn us but will instead guide us toward transformation. The apostle Paul urges believers to come to God with humble hearts, admitting their weaknesses, and receiving His grace. In 2 Corinthians 12:9 (NIV), Paul recounts God's response to his struggles, *"But he said to me, 'My grace is sufficient for you, for my power is made perfect in weakness.' Therefore I will boast all the more gladly of my weaknesses, so that the power of Christ may rest upon me."* This openness allows God's grace to work in us, turning our weaknesses into opportunities for His strength.

Ultimately, spiritual openness before God enhances our relationship with Him. It deepens the connection between the believer and their Creator, removing barriers like pride or self-reliance that can obstruct genuine intimacy. In James 4:8 (NIV), we are invited to draw near to God: *"Come near to God and he will come near to you. Wash your hands, you sinners, and purify your hearts, you double-minded."* This verse encourages believers to purify their hearts and approach God without pretense, knowing that He will meet them with love and understanding. When we embrace spiritual openness, we experience the beauty of being fully known and fully loved by the God who created us, which fosters a deeper, more authentic faith journey.

EMBRACING VULNERABILITY: THE POWER OF OPENNESS IN GOD'S PRESENCE

Spiritual nakedness, when understood in the context of God's presence, invites believers to surrender all pretenses and embrace vulnerability before Him. In Psalm 139:7-10, NIV, the psalmist acknowledges the omnipresence and omniscience of God, reminding us that no matter where we go, God's presence is with us. *"Where can I go from your Spirit? Where can I flee from your presence?"* These words remind us that God sees beyond our external actions and understands our hearts fully. Nakedness, in this sense, means being honest with God, knowing that we cannot hide anything from Him. It requires us to come before Him not as people with perfected lives but as those who acknowledge their flaws, imperfections, and dependence on His grace.

The example of Jonah further illustrates the depth of this transparency. Jonah, fleeing from God's command, thought he could escape God's presence by boarding a ship and traveling in the opposite direction. Yet, in the belly of the fish, Jonah could not escape God. His prayer, though from the depths of despair, was heard by God. This illustrates that God is ever-present, even in the lowest points of our lives. Jonah's willingness to confess his wrongdoing and seek God's mercy in his vulnerable state led to his deliverance. It shows that spiritual nakedness is not about avoiding failure or sin but about being open to God's grace and seeking His help when we are most exposed and vulnerable.

Hebrews 4:13 also reinforces this concept by reminding us that nothing is hidden from God's sight: *"Nothing in all creation is hidden from God's sight. Everything is uncovered and laid bare before the eyes of him to whom we must give account."* Spiritual nakedness requires believers to live with this awareness that God sees and understands every part of our lives. This truth may initially feel uncomfortable, as it calls for full exposure, but it is a call to honesty and humility before the Creator. Trying to hide our faults or wear a mask of perfection only prevents the deep, transformative relationship God desires with us. It is only through honesty that we can experience true intimacy with Him.

Christian author A.W. Tozer once said, "We must learn to live with the truth that God sees everything about us." This perspective shifts our mindset from shame and fear of exposure to the peace that comes from knowing that God desires honesty and transparency. Instead of hiding our brokenness, we can offer it to God, trusting in His grace and mercy. This vulnerability allows for a deeper connection with God, as it removes the barriers that often hinder our spiritual growth. When we are exposed before God, we are inviting His healing presence into the areas of our hearts that need transformation.

Ultimately, spiritual nakedness before God invites believers to live authentically. It is not an act of humiliation or shame but of surrender and trust in God's ability to guide and transform us. This openness and vulnerability before God set the stage for His work in our lives. By acknowledging our flaws and seeking His will, we create a space for God to shape us more into His likeness. As we live in this vulnerable state, we will see our faith grow deeper and more authentic. This call to spiritual nakedness is not just for the present but is a lifelong journey, reminding us to continuously surrender our hearts to God and trust in His transforming power.

Embracing spiritual nakedness is about acknowledging that God knows us completely and invites us to live in openness and vulnerability before Him. It challenges us to abandon pretense and trust in His grace to transform us. Just as Jonah's vulnerable prayer was answered, so too does God respond to hearts that humbly seek Him. As we live in this vulnerability, we experience greater intimacy with God, allowing His will to shape our lives. This call to openness serves as a powerful reminder for believers to live authentically in the presence of God.

NAKEDNESS AS A SYMBOL OF RENEWAL AND TRANSFORMATION

The Bible often illustrates renewal and transformation through the shedding of old garments or identities to embrace the new. This act of removal signifies a spiritual transition letting go of past limitations or sins to step into a new phase of life guided by faith. Let`s consider the following scenarios;

i. Joseph's Transformation: A Symbol of Readiness for God's Plan

Joseph's transformation in Genesis 41:14 marks a pivotal moment in his life. When Pharaoh summoned him, Joseph was still in prison clothes, a symbol of his current status as a prisoner. However, he deliberately removed his prison garments and shaved before appearing before Pharaoh. This act was not just about appearance; it was an intentional step of preparing himself mentally, emotionally, and spiritually for the new role that God had destined for him. Genesis 41:14 (NIV) states, *"So Pharaoh sent for Joseph, and he was quickly brought from the dungeon. When he had shaved and changed his clothes, he came before Pharaoh."* Joseph's willingness to change his appearance reflected his readiness to step into the new purpose God had prepared for him.

Joseph's shedding of his prison garments symbolizes his willingness to leave behind his past and embrace the future that God had planned for him. Throughout his trials, Joseph remained faithful to God, despite being betrayed by his brothers and unjustly imprisoned. The act of removing his prison attire was a symbolic gesture of letting go of the shame and bitterness that could have hindered his progress. It was a physical manifestation of the internal transformation that had occurred in his heart. This change highlights the importance of being spiritually ready to step into the purpose God has for us. Just as Joseph had to release his old identity to embrace his new role, we too must be willing to let go of past hurts, failures, or doubts to fully embrace what God has prepared for us.

This transformation can also be understood as an act of faith. Joseph's decision to change his clothes and appearance was a statement of belief in God's sovereignty and the new role he was about to assume. He did not allow his circumstances, such as his time in prison, to define him. Rather, he chose to align himself with God's vision for his future. The act of preparation demonstrated that Joseph believed God had a greater plan for him than the one he had been living in. In the same way, when we trust in God's plan for our lives, we can begin to act in faith, preparing ourselves for what He is calling us to, even if it seems beyond our current situation.

Joseph's transformation also serves as a reminder for believers to recognize and seize moments of divine opportunity. When Joseph appeared before Pharaoh, he was not just offering his wisdom; he was stepping into a leadership role that would save nations and fulfill God's promise. Christian author and speaker Joyce Meyer often emphasizes, *"God doesn't just want to change your circumstances; He wants to change you."* Joseph's change in attire and demeanor was a reflection of that internal change that allowed him to rise to the occasion. This teaches us that when God calls us to a new season or purpose, we must be ready, not only externally but internally, prepared for the transformation He has planned. Are we willing to shed our old selves and step into the fullness of what God has for us, trusting that He is with us every step of the way?

ii. Bartimaeus' Faith: Abandoning the Old for a New Identity

The story of Bartimaeus, the blind beggar, is a profound illustration of faith and transformation. In Mark 10:50 (NIV), when Jesus called Bartimaeus, *"Throwing his cloak aside, he jumped to his feet and came to Jesus."* The act of casting aside his cloak was not merely a physical gesture, but a symbolic act of abandoning his old identity. The cloak he wore represented his condition as a beggar his blindness and reliance on others for survival. By removing it, Bartimaeus was not just preparing himself to approach Jesus physically, but also spiritually preparing to receive healing and a new identity. It was a declaration of faith that he would no longer remain in his past condition but would step forward into the new life Jesus had for him.

Bartimaeus' action reflects a deep trust in Jesus' ability to transform his life. His cloak was an essential part of his identity as a beggar people would recognize him by it. Yet, when he heard Jesus calling him, he immediately threw aside that symbol of his past. This abandonment of his cloak illustrates his willingness to step away from everything that defined his old life. Jesus, seeing his faith, responded by healing him. In the same way, when we encounter Jesus, we are called to lay aside the things that hinder our spiritual progress whether they be past hurts, doubts, or old habits—and move toward the new identity He offers. As Christian author Max Lucado states, "Faith is not just a belief; it is a willingness to act."

The significance of Bartimaeus' action goes beyond the physical act of casting away his cloak. It serves as a challenge to us: are we willing to let go of the identities and limitations that define us? Do we cling to our past failures, fears, or disappointments, or are we ready to take a step of faith and embrace the transformative power of Jesus? Bartimaeus' faith wasn't passive; it was an active response to the call of Jesus. When Jesus called him, he didn't hesitate he didn't wait to see if healing would be immediate. His response was full of trust that Jesus could and would change his life. How often do we hold on to our doubts or past experiences, unwilling to let them go and fully trust in God's power to transform?

Bartimaeus' faith ultimately led to his healing, but it also marked the beginning of his new identity in Christ. When Jesus asked him, *"What do you want me to do for you?"* (Mark 10:51 NIV), Bartimaeus didn't ask for wealth or status; he asked for sight. His request was not selfish but rooted in a desire for restoration and wholeness. Once healed, he didn't return to his old life as a beggar but followed Jesus along the road (Mark 10:52). This represents the life-changing impact of true faith. When we respond to Jesus with faith, casting aside our old selves, we are transformed and invited into a new identity and purpose. In the words of Christian author C.S. Lewis, *"Faith is the art of holding on to things your reason has once accepted, in spite of your changing moods."* Bartimaeus demonstrated that kind of unwavering faith, showing us the power of casting aside the old to embrace the new in Christ.

THE CONCEPT OF SHEDDING THE OLD IN RELATIONSHIPS

In relationships, particularly marriage, the idea of shedding old burdens and embracing a renewed mindset is essential for growth and transformation. Just as individuals enter into marriage with the desire to build a strong, committed partnership, they must be willing to leave behind past baggage, unresolved hurts, and harmful behaviors. These emotional or spiritual burdens can hinder the ability to truly connect and nurture a healthy relationship. The Bible speaks to this process of transformation, urging believers to let go of the old and embrace the new, both in their personal lives and in their relationships. In Ephesians 4:22-24 (NIV), Paul writes, *"You were taught, with regard to your former way of life, to put off your old self, which is being corrupted by its deceitful desires; to be made new in the attitude of your minds; and to put on the new self, created to be like God in true righteousness and holiness."* This passage highlights the necessity of abandoning the old self in order to embrace a new way of living, rooted in righteousness and holiness.

In marriage, this shedding process requires vulnerability and openness, mirroring the spiritual concept of nakedness. Just as one would not enter into a relationship with a façade or a mask, the same is true for our spiritual lives. The willingness to expose one's vulnerabilities whether past hurts, insecurities, or weaknesses creates space for growth and healing. This process requires deep trust in God's plan and a willingness to surrender the past, knowing that He has a purpose for our lives that far exceeds anything we could imagine. Christian author Gary Thomas writes, "The essence of marriage is not to create a perfect partnership but to learn to become better partners for each other by shedding our old ways and becoming more like Christ." This means choosing to embrace God's transformative work in our lives, even when it requires letting go of painful past experiences or ingrained habits.

This renewal and transformation, both in relationships and in our spiritual journey, are acts of obedience and faith. As individuals allow God to reshape their identities, they become better equipped for the roles and blessings He has in store for them. Marriage, like any other covenant, is a process of continual growth and renewal. Through spiritual nakedness, we expose ourselves before God and allow His grace to enter, making us more attuned to His will. The key question is: Are we willing to shed our old selves the burdens of past mistakes and hurts to embrace the new identity that God offers? It is only by allowing ourselves to be reshaped and remade in His image that we can fully experience the fullness of life, not just spiritually but in our relationships as well. As Christian author Tim Keller says, *"In marriage, you give up your right to live your own life."* By embracing God's plan and surrendering our past, we make room for a transformed future, one that aligns with His will and purpose.

NAKEDNESS AS CONTENTMENT AND GRATITUDE

Nakedness before God calls believers to recognize Him as the ultimate source of life and all blessings. This acknowledgement fosters a spirit of contentment and gratitude, encouraging us to appreciate what we have rather than focusing on what we lack. When we are spiritually naked before God, we are vulnerable enough to accept His provision and recognize that everything we have comes from His hand. It challenges us to resist the distractions that often lead to dissatisfaction, urging us to find contentment in God alone. In 1 Timothy 6:6-8 (NIV), Paul writes, *"But godliness with contentment is great gain. For we brought nothing into the world, and we can take nothing out of it. But if we have food and clothing, we will be content with that."* This passage reminds us that true contentment comes from recognizing the sufficiency of God's provision, not from accumulating more possessions or achievements.

Scripture frequently emphasizes the importance of contentment and gratitude, urging believers to trust in God's provision rather than coveting what others have. Ecclesiastes 5:19 (NIV) highlights this principle, stating, *"When God gives someone wealth and possessions, and the ability to enjoy them, to accept their lot and be happy in their toil this is a gift of God."* The verse underscores the truth that contentment is not about striving for more but learning to appreciate and enjoy what God has already given. Christian author John Piper writes, *"Contentment is not the fulfillment of what you want, but the realization of how much you already have."* This perspective shifts our focus from the constant pursuit of more to the gratitude and satisfaction found in what God has already provided.

Nakedness before God also involves cultivating a heart of gratitude, which changes the way we see our circumstances. Gratitude allows us to recognize God's hand in every aspect of our lives, no matter how small or seemingly insignificant. When we approach life with a grateful heart, we stop comparing ourselves to others and begin to appreciate the sufficiency of God's provision. As Paul writes in Philippians 4:11-12 (NIV), *"I have learned to be content whatever the circumstances. I know what it is to be in need, and I know what it is to have plenty."* Paul's example shows us that contentment is a learned attitude, not dependent on our external circumstances but on our internal trust in God's faithfulness. Are we willing to embrace this attitude of contentment, trusting that

God knows what is best for us and that His provision is always enough? As Christian author Ann Voskamp reminds us, *"Gratitude always has the power to change the atmosphere of our hearts and lives."* When we cultivate a heart of gratitude, we find joy in what we have, knowing that God's provision is always sufficient.

Furthermore, the pursuit of unnecessary distractions whether material, emotional, or spiritual often stems from a lack of contentment. These pursuits can cloud our vision, leading us away from God's purposes and creating a sense of inadequacy. Nakedness calls us to strip away these distractions, focusing instead on the essentials of our faith and the blessings God has already provided. Jesus teaches this in Matthew 6:33, NIV: *"But seek first His kingdom and His righteousness, and all these things will be given to you as well."* Ultimately, nakedness before God is an invitation to live in simplicity and trust, embracing contentment and gratitude as central elements of a life devoted to Him. It is a posture of humility that acknowledges God's provision and seeks to align our desires with His will. By doing so, believers can experience the joy and peace that come from a heart fully surrendered to God's care and guidance.

NAKEDNESS AS TOTAL SURRENDER AND OPENNESS IN RELATIONSHIPS

Nakedness in relationships represents total surrender and openness, where individuals expose their true selves without fear of rejection or judgment. This level of vulnerability requires a deep trust, as it calls for abandoning pretense and embracing authenticity, allowing the relationship to be built on truth and mutual respect. In marriage, this is particularly important, as it mirrors the way God desires His relationship with us one of complete openness and surrender. Ephesians 5:31 (NIV) states, *"For this reason a man will leave his father and mother and be united to his wife, and the two will become one flesh."* This unity symbolizes a deep, selfless connection where both individuals give their whole selves to each other. Christian author Tim Keller writes, "In marriage, the union of two people becomes a model of the intimacy between Christ and His church." Are we willing to fully surrender our fears, insecurities, and past hurts in our relationships, trusting that God's grace will cover our vulnerabilities? True openness in relationships doesn't come from perfection but from a willingness to be transparent and real, acknowledging that only through God's grace can we experience genuine intimacy.

Nakedness symbolizes complete surrender and openness, particularly in relationships whether with God or with one another. At creation, God presented Adam and Eve to each other in their natural, unadorned state, with no barriers, pretense, or reservations. This act exemplified ultimate vulnerability and trust, laying the foundation for relationships built on honesty, mutual dependence, and authentic connection. In this state of nakedness, Adam and Eve were able to embrace each other fully, without fear or shame.

The idea of nakedness in relationships reflects the call to live without emotional or spiritual barriers. It invites individuals to be transparent, to offer their true selves without hiding behind facades. This is the kind of openness that God desires not only in our relationship with Him but also in how we interact with others. As Christians, we are called to lay aside any falsehoods or guardedness in relationships, striving for honesty, trust, and vulnerability. Just as Adam and Eve were presented to each other in their unadorned state, we too should offer ourselves freely, unmasked, and without pretense, especially in marriage.

In marriage, for example, the call to "be all in" with one another reflects the kind of surrender and trust that God intended. A couple that is open, willing to be vulnerable and transparent with each other, is better able to weather the storms of life. However, this openness cannot be passive; it requires ongoing communication, selflessness, and the willingness to address hurts and misunderstandings as they arise. Ultimately, nakedness in relationships is a call to remove the walls we often build to protect ourselves and to instead trust God and each other fully. It is a commitment to love, honor, and be vulnerable in the truest sense, reflecting the perfect example of love demonstrated by God in Christ.

NAKEDNESS AND THE EFFORT REQUIRED FOR TRANSFORMATION

The idea that "everything is workable" is rooted in the truth that we must be willing to invest the necessary effort. In relationships, whether it's marriage, friendships, or our walk with God, nothing works automatically. It requires active participation and determination. The concept of nakedness in this context symbolizes humility the willingness to recognize imperfections and the commitment to continue working, even when faced with challenges.

In marriage, for instance, couples often experience difficult times when the issues seem overwhelming. It is easy to think, *"This is too hard; it's not working."* However, the reality is that relationships can work if both parties are committed and proactive. The struggles may not simply disappear on their own, but with patience, communication, and mutual effort, they can be overcome. Likewise, in our spiritual journey, growth and fulfilment do not occur passively. Without consistent prayer, studying God's word, and depending on Him, spiritual development remains stagnant. We cannot expect to draw closer to God if we are not intentional about making the effort to seek Him.

Nakedness, in this case, can be understood as surrendering our own will and embracing the humility to admit our limitations. Just as Adam and Eve's nakedness represented vulnerability and trust before God, we too must be willing to expose our flaws and acknowledge our need for God's guidance. Life's difficulties, whether relational or personal, are navigated best when we rely on His strength, recognizing that we cannot face these challenges alone.

This surrender to God's will is not about passivity but about embracing an active dependence on Him. It's about recognizing that we cannot do it all ourselves, and that through His strength, we are equipped to persevere. Whether in relationships or personal struggles, the key to making things work is not avoiding effort but embracing it. Through humility, faith, and perseverance, everything is workable.

NAKEDNESS AS A THIRST FOR GOD'S SPIRIT

Nakedness, in the spiritual sense, represents a deep yearning for God's presence and a thirst for His Spirit that transcends the distractions and superficial pursuits of this world. In a culture where success, wealth, and material gain often promise fulfillment but ultimately leave a void, spiritual nakedness calls us to acknowledge that only through God can we experience true peace and purpose. Without God, our best efforts feel futile, like trying to fill an infinite gap with temporary solutions. As Psalm 42:1-2 (NIV) states, *"As the deer pants for streams of water, so my soul pants for you, my God. My soul thirsts for God, for the living God."* The psalmist captures the essence of spiritual nakedness a deep, unwavering thirst for God's presence. This longing reflects a heart that recognizes its dependence on God for both spiritual direction and personal fulfillment. Are we so thirsty for God's Spirit that we are willing to lay down every distraction and pursuit that hinders our relationship with Him?

When Adam first saw Eve, he expressed profound joy at the beauty and completeness of God's creation. His recognition of her as *"bone of my bones"* and *"flesh of my flesh"* (Genesis 2:23) was a moment of purity, untainted by the selfishness or corruption that often distorts relationships. This moment of nakedness was not just physical but spiritual, as it symbolized the perfect, unbroken communion God intended for His creation. In the same way, spiritual nakedness calls us to embrace a newness in our relationship with God a fresh start where we shed the burdens of past distractions and refocus our hearts on what matters most: His presence. Jesus teaches us in Matthew 5:6 (NIV), *"Blessed are those who hunger and thirst for righteousness, for they will be filled."* Just as Adam found completeness in God's creation, we find spiritual renewal and satisfaction in seeking His righteousness.

Spiritual nakedness means acknowledging our total dependence on God. It invites us to lay bare our hearts before Him, acknowledging that without His Spirit, our lives are incomplete and our efforts insufficient. Jesus, in John 15:5 (NIV), reminds us, *"I am the vine; you are the branches. If you remain in me and I in you, you will bear much fruit; apart from me you can do nothing."* The truth of this verse highlights the necessity of God's presence in every aspect of our lives. Without Him, our labor is in vain, and we can never fully experience the fulfillment He offers. Are we willing to live in complete dependence on God, trusting that only through His Spirit can we bear fruit and live a life that truly matters?

Nakedness, in this context, is also a call to hunger for God's Spirit and to desire His constant renewal. In a world that offers temporary solutions and fleeting pleasures, God's Spirit is the only source of lasting transformation and peace. Galatians 5:22-23 (NIV) describes the fruits of the Spirit, including love, joy, peace, forbearance, kindness, goodness, faithfulness, gentleness, and self-control. These qualities cannot be manufactured through human effort alone; they are the natural result of a life lived in the fullness of God's presence. As we embrace spiritual nakedness, we invite God's Spirit to guide us, transform us, and make us more like Christ. Do we truly hunger for this transformation, or have we allowed the distractions of the world to diminish our desire for the Spirit's work in our lives?

So, spiritual nakedness and thirsting for God's Spirit lead us to a place of restoration and fulfilment. It is only by aligning ourselves with God's will and inviting His presence that we can experience the transformation He desires for us. Psalm 63:1 (NIV) expresses this beautifully: *"You, God, are my God, earnestly I seek you; I thirst for you, my whole being longs for you, in a dry and parched land where there is no water."* This yearning is not just for physical needs but for a deeper, spiritual connection with God. It is through this longing that our souls are restored, and our lives are filled with purpose and joy. Are we willing to enter into this profound thirst for God's Spirit, allowing Him to shape us into the people He has called us to be?

NOTE THESE

Contentment comes from God's provision – True fulfilment is found in recognizing and appreciating what God has already given rather than striving for more.

Gratitude transforms perspective – A heart of gratitude helps believers focus on God's sufficiency rather than comparing themselves to others.

Openness fosters stronger relationships – Vulnerability and honesty in relationships lead to deeper connections, just as God desires full surrender from His people.

Spiritual growth requires effort – Transformation and intimacy with God demand intentional pursuit, prayer, and dependence on Him.

A thirst for God leads to true fulfilment – Only by seeking God's Spirit can we experience lasting peace, joy, and purpose in life.

CHAPTER ELEVEN

DISCERNMENT IN RELATIONSHIPS AND COMMITMENT

Nakedness in relationships encompasses the vital role of discernment. In any relationship be it romantic, friendship, or professional there are often subtle signs that indicate whether the connection is healthy or heading toward difficulty. These signs are frequently sensed early on, but many tend to ignore them, hoping for change or improvement with time. Nakedness in relationships calls for the courage to embrace clarity and honesty about the true nature of the relationship, even when it's uncomfortable. In John 8:32 (NIV), Jesus tells us, *"Then you will know the truth, and the truth will set you free."* This passage highlights the importance of being truthful in our assessments of relationships. Are we willing to face the truth, even when it's difficult, and allow God to guide our actions?

Often in relationships that eventually end in disappointment or pain, both individuals experience a sense of unease early on. It's a gut feeling or an intuitive warning that something is amiss, yet these feelings are often dismissed in the hope that things will improve with time or effort. However, ignoring these early signs can lead to more profound frustration and heartache down the road. Proverbs 2:11 (NIV) says, *"Discretion will protect you, and understanding will guard you."* This verse reminds us that discernment and wisdom serve as protective measures in our relationships, helping us navigate through potential pitfalls before they become larger issues. How many times do we push aside our intuition, thinking we can control the outcome, only to find that those initial warnings were signs of something deeper?

Spiritual nakedness, in the context of relationships, is not just about being vulnerable; it is also about cultivating discernment. It requires being honest with ourselves and others, recognizing and acknowledging the truths that may be difficult to confront. Discernment in relationships calls us to assess not just the superficial qualities of a person, but also the deeper, foundational aspects such as character, values, and goals. Hebrews 5:14 (NIV) speaks to this need for discernment: *"But solid food is for the mature, who by constant use have trained themselves to distinguish good from evil."* As we grow in spiritual maturity, we are better equipped to discern what aligns with God's will for our lives, allowing us to make decisions that honor Him and lead to healthier, more fulfilling relationships.

The clarity gained through discernment allows us to avoid unnecessary emotional turmoil. When we acknowledge the truth of a situation early, we can act accordingly whether that means addressing an issue directly, setting healthy boundaries, or even walking away from a relationship that is not aligned with God's purposes. Nakedness in relationships means recognizing that not all relationships are meant to last or to thrive. Ecclesiastes 3:1 (NIV) reminds us that *"There is a time for everything, and a season for every activity under the heavens."* Discernment helps us understand the season we are in and whether a relationship is contributing positively to our lives or hindering our growth. Are we truly listening to the signals around us, or are we ignoring them in the hopes of avoiding discomfort?

Hence, relationships built on discernment and clarity are those that grow in alignment with God's principles. When we approach relationships with the intention of fostering mutual understanding, trust, and commitment, we create an environment where both parties can thrive in the fullness of God's plan. Colossians 3:14 (NIV) encourages us *to "And over all these virtues put on love, which binds them all together in perfect unity."* This verse emphasizes that when discernment and honesty are at the heart of a relationship, love becomes the foundation that holds everything together. By practicing discernment, we are better able to enter into relationships that align with God's will, leading to greater joy, peace, and fulfillment. Are we committed to discerning God's purpose in our relationships and allowing Him to guide us in making choices that honor Him?

LIVING IN NAKEDNESS BEFORE GOD AND OTHERS

Nakedness, both spiritually and relationally, serves as a profound call to vulnerability, humility, and authenticity. In its deepest form, it encourages us to live transparently before both God and others, acknowledging our weaknesses and imperfections without hiding behind facades. This concept of living in nakedness can be traced back to the beginning of creation when Adam and Eve were introduced to each other in their natural, unguarded state (Genesis 2:25, NIV: *"Adam and his wife were both naked, and they felt no shame"*). In the context of our walk with God, spiritual nakedness involves the willingness to lay bare our hearts before Him, free from pride and pretense. As author Tim Keller once said, *"To be loved but not known is comforting, but superficial. To be known and not loved is our greatest fear. But to be fully known and truly loved is, well, a lot like being loved by God."* This highlights the importance of living openly before God, knowing that He sees us fully yet loves us completely.

In our relationship with God, spiritual nakedness calls us to strip away the layers that often keep us from true intimacy with Him pride, fear, and self-reliance. These barriers prevent us from fully experiencing God's presence and grace. Jesus invites us to come to Him without pretense, acknowledging our complete dependence on Him. In James 4:10 (NIV), we are told, *"Humble yourselves before the Lord, and he will lift you up."* This humility is essential for growth and transformation. Are we willing to surrender our false sense of self-sufficiency and approach God with an open heart, allowing Him to reveal our hidden fears and desires? Only through this vulnerability can we experience the fullness of His love and mercy, transforming our lives from the inside out.

Living in nakedness before others, much like with God, requires the willingness to expose ourselves without the defense of pride or masks. In relationships, whether with friends, family, or a spouse, being emotionally and spiritually naked means trusting others with our true selves our flaws, struggles, and weaknesses. This act of vulnerability is not a sign of weakness, but one of strength. As Brené Brown, a well-known researcher on vulnerability, writes, *"Vulnerability is not winning or losing; it's having the courage to show up and be seen when we have no control over the outcome."* This courage to be seen as we truly are allows for deeper, more authentic connections with others. In relationships that are built on this kind of vulnerability, there is a mutual understanding and a bond that transcends superficial interactions.

Therefore, living in nakedness before God and others leads us to a life of greater fulfilment, peace, and joy. By embracing this transparency and surrender, we open ourselves to the transformative power of God's grace. In Ephesians 5:8 (NIV), we are reminded: *"For you were once darkness, but now you are light in the Lord. Live as children of light."* This invitation calls us to live in the light, allowing God to purify our hearts and guide us in every relationship. While this process requires ongoing effort, commitment, and a willingness to surrender our own desires, it is through these acts of spiritual and relational nakedness that we are transformed. Living fully exposed in God's grace leads to lasting peace, joy, and a deeper connection with those around us. Are we ready to live openly, trusting God to guide us toward deeper, more meaningful relationships with Him and others?

UNITY IN MARRIAGE: "BONE OF MY BONE AND FLESH OF MY FLESH"

Adam's declaration, *"Bone of my bone and flesh of my flesh"* (Genesis 2:23, NIV), speaks to the deep unity and sacredness of marriage. This statement is more than a poetic expression; it reveals the profound and intrinsic connection that God intended for a husband and wife. When Adam recognized Eve as part of himself, he acknowledged that their union was not merely a social contract but a divine act that reflected God's image. In marriage, there is an inseparable bond, a deep unity where two individuals become one in spirit, soul, and body. This is not a physical union alone, but a spiritual and emotional one, where the two become interconnected in a way that goes beyond mere companionship.

The significance of this union is also highlighted in the New Testament, where Paul reinforces the idea of becoming one flesh in Ephesians 5:31 (NIV), stating, *"For this reason a man will leave his father and mother and be united to his wife, and the two will become one flesh."* This emphasizes that the marital relationship is a covenant that transcends all other relationships, grounded in love, sacrifice, and mutual respect. The metaphor of "bone of my bone and flesh of my flesh" indicates the shared essence of the marriage relationship. It asks the question: how often do we, in our marriages, recognize the deep interconnectedness of our spouse as someone who is intricately tied to our being? Are we living in such a way that reflects the sacredness and unity that God intended?

Christian author Gary Thomas, in his book *Sacred Marriage*, explores the idea that marriage is not just about personal happiness but about reflecting God's purpose for mankind. He writes, *"What if God designed marriage to make us holy more than to make us happy?"* This statement invites us to reconsider the purpose of unity in marriage, suggesting that the true calling is to grow together in holiness and righteousness, reflecting the unity found in Christ. It challenges us to view marriage not just as a relationship to fulfill personal needs but as a sacred bond that shapes our spiritual lives. This unity, rooted in God's design, requires commitment, sacrifice, and the willingness to serve one another, just as Christ serves His Church.

In practical terms, living out the unity described in Genesis 2:23 requires ongoing effort and intentionality. How often do we allow external pressures, misunderstandings, or selfish desires to create division in our marriages? Unity in marriage isn't about avoiding conflict but about being willing to work through challenges together, always remembering the foundational truth that we are "bone of my bone and flesh of my flesh." In Philippians 2:3-4 (NIV), Paul reminds us, *"Do nothing out of selfish ambition or vain conceit. Rather, in humility value others above yourselves, not looking to your own interests but each of you to the interests of the others."* This posture of humility and selflessness is key to nurturing the unity God desires for marriages. Are we consistently choosing to prioritize our spouse's needs, recognizing that their well-being is intimately connected to our own?

ADAM'S COMMITMENT TO EVE

Adam's commitment to Eve, particularly in the context of the Fall, speaks volumes about the depth of his devotion to her. In Genesis 3:6 (NIV), we read that after Eve ate the forbidden fruit, *"she also gave some to her husband, who was with her, and he ate it."* Adam's decision to eat the fruit, despite knowing it was against God's command, reveals the depth of his connection to Eve. In this moment, Adam's devotion to Eve took precedence over his obedience to God. This act of choosing Eve over divine instruction highlights the profound bond between them, a bond that transcended mere partnership and entered into the realm of deep emotional and spiritual unity. Even though his action had dire consequences, it demonstrates how strongly Adam identified with Eve, she was not just his partner but a vital extension of himself, as seen in his earlier declaration, "Bone of my bone and flesh of my flesh" (Genesis 2:23).

This deep connection between Adam and Eve underscores the biblical understanding of marriage as a union where both individuals are not just companions but are intricately woven together in a shared purpose and commitment. Jesus, in Matthew 19:5 (NIV), echoes this when He says, *"For this reason a man will leave his father and mother and be united to his wife, and the two will become one flesh."* This highlights that marriage is not merely a social contract but a sacred covenant. Adam's choice to align with Eve, even at the cost of disobeying God, reflects this level of commitment where the unity of the relationship takes precedence over individual interest. How often do we, in our relationships, place the well-being of our spouse above all else, even when it's inconvenient or difficult?

Christian author Timothy Keller, in his book *The Meaning of Marriage*, speaks to this profound commitment: *"Marriage is the biggest mirror in the world because it reflects what we are like with God."* Keller emphasizes that marriage requires sacrificial love, just as Christ sacrificed for His Church. Adam's choice, though flawed, provides a glimpse of the sacrificial love that marriage calls for. It challenges us to think about how committed we are to our spouses are we willing to make sacrifices for their well-being, even when it's difficult? Adam's act of disobedience was driven by his love and commitment to Eve, but as Christians, we are called to reflect sacrificial love that is grounded in obedience to God, as modeled by Christ.

The consequences of Adam's decision in the garden serve as a sobering reminder of the importance of commitment in relationships. While the bond between Adam and Eve was strong, their actions led to the fall of humanity, showing that decisions made within a relationship can have far-reaching effects. This highlights the responsibility that comes with the commitment we make to our spouses. In Ephesians 5:25 (NIV), Paul instructs husbands to *"love your wives, just as Christ loved the church and gave himself up for her."* Adam's decision in the garden reminds us of the importance of making choices that honor both our spouse and God. Are we making decisions that strengthen the unity and health of our marriages, or are we allowing our actions to drive wedges between us and our loved ones? Adam's commitment, though imperfect, serves as a powerful lesson on the depth and responsibility that comes with marriage.

THE WISDOM OF UNITY

Unity in marriage is more than simply existing together; it requires a deliberate decision to value the partnership over personal dominance or superficial desires. In Genesis 2:24 (NIV), we are told, *"That is why a man leaves his father and mother and is united to his wife, and they become one flesh."* This divine command shows that marriage is about two individuals coming together to form a unified whole, where each person complements and supports the other. Adam's acceptance of Eve as his "bone of my bones and flesh of my flesh" (Genesis 2:23) signifies not only an emotional and physical bond but also a spiritual and intellectual partnership. In marriage, we are called to honor and value our spouse, placing the relationship above our own personal desires. The wisdom of unity lies in recognizing that the strength of a marriage is found in mutual respect, love, and collaboration, not in the pursuit of individual dominance or selfish gain.

This wisdom challenges couples today to consider how they view their relationships. Are we focused on controlling or winning, or are we more concerned with nurturing the unity between us? In many marriages, pride and self-interest can disrupt the harmony that God intends. Christian author Gary Chapman, in his book *The 5 Love Languages*, emphasizes that love is an action, a decision to serve and care for one another, not just a feeling. True unity in marriage requires selflessness, where both partners seek the best for each other, not just for themselves. It's a partnership that calls for mutual sacrifice, as Christ demonstrated through His relationship with the Church. How often do we approach marriage with a spirit of humility and love, eager to serve and support our spouse?

Adam's example also demonstrates that true leadership in marriage is rooted in love and unity. Leadership doesn't mean control; it means sacrificially protecting and guiding the relationship. In Ephesians 5:25 (NIV), Paul instructs husbands to *"love your wives, just as Christ loved the church and gave himself up for her."* This is not a directive to dominate but to lead with sacrificial love, putting the needs of the wife first. Leadership in marriage is about cultivating an environment of mutual respect and care. It is not about enforcing one's will but rather seeking to understand and support each other in every way. The wisdom of unity involves a leadership that cherishes and protects the sacredness of the marriage covenant. Do we lead with love and humility, recognizing that our role is to build up our spouse, not to exert control over them?

Women, too, are called to honor the wisdom of unity in their relationships. The Bible encourages wives to respect their husbands and recognize their leadership (Ephesians 5:33). This doesn't mean blind obedience or subservience but rather an acknowledgement of the complementary roles within the marriage. A healthy marriage is based on a deep respect for each other's strengths and contributions. When both partners embrace the wisdom of unity where love, respect, and mutual care are the foundations they form a strong and enduring bond. As Christian author Tim Keller writes in *The Meaning of Marriage*, "Marriage is a union in which a husband and wife honor, cherish, and serve each other for the glory of God." The question for couples is: Do we approach marriage with the understanding that unity requires effort, sacrifice, and mutual respect, or do we focus on our own desires, causing division? True unity is a reflection of God's design and a testament to His love for His people.

NOTE THESE

Commitment Requires Sacrifice – Adam's choice demonstrates that deep relationships often demand difficult sacrifices, but they should be guided by obedience to God.

Marriage is a Sacred Covenant – The bond between Adam and Eve highlights that marriage is not just a partnership but a divine unity ordained by God.

Decisions in Marriage Have Consequences – Adam's decision to prioritize Eve over God's command led to serious repercussions, teaching that choices in relationships carry lasting effects.

True Leadership in Marriage is Rooted in Love – Biblical leadership is about sacrificial love and protection, not control or dominance.

Unity Requires Mutual Respect and Humility – A strong marriage is built on selflessness, where both partners honor, support, and serve each other.

CHAPTER TWELVE

HEALING IN RELATIONSHIPS

The analogy of a broken bone offers an insightful picture of how relationships can experience healing and restoration in times of trouble. Just as the body doesn't abandon a broken bone but works to heal it, so too should we approach broken relationships with the same resilience and commitment. In Ephesians 4:32 (NIV), the Apostle Paul urges believers, *"Be kind and compassionate to one another, forgiving each other, just as in Christ God forgave you."* Healing in relationships often requires deep forgiveness, humility, and a willingness to work through pain rather than avoid or abandon it. This process may take time and effort, but like the body's natural response to injury, it is essential for the restoration of the relationship.

In relationships, particularly marriages or close friendships, challenges will inevitably arise. These challenges can be emotional, relational, or even spiritual, causing fractures that may feel overwhelming. However, healing is not about running from the problem but about leaning into the discomfort with a commitment to restoration. Christian author Dr. Gary Chapman, in his book *The Five Love Languages*, emphasizes the importance of understanding and addressing the emotional needs of each partner. He writes, *"The willingness to forgive is an essential part of emotional healing."* Healing, like the repair of a broken bone, requires time, intentionality, and a heart that is open to the process of restoration. Do we approach our relationships with the mindset of healing, or are we quick to abandon them when difficulties arise?

The Bible teaches that true healing in relationships comes through the power of reconciliation. In 2 Corinthians 5:18 (NIV), Paul writes, *"All this is from God, who reconciled us to himself through Christ and gave us the ministry of reconciliation."* Just as God restored our broken relationship with Him through Christ, He calls us to seek reconciliation with one another. Healing in relationships isn't just about addressing the immediate issue; it is about restoring the connection and rebuilding trust over time. This process often involves honest communication, empathy, and a willingness to grow together. When we face relational challenges, are we seeking reconciliation, or are we allowing bitterness and division to take root?

So, healing in relationships requires a steadfast commitment to one another. It's easy to give up when the going gets tough, but God calls us to be faithful and dedicated in our relationships. In Romans 12:10 (NIV), Paul exhorts us, *"Be devoted to one another in love. Honor one another above yourselves."* This kind of devotion doesn't waver in the face of difficulty; it is a deep-rooted commitment to nurturing and protecting the relationship. Healing requires both parties to commit to the long process of restoration, holding onto love and faith even when things seem broken. Do we view our relationships as worth fighting for, even when healing seems like a long journey? The resilience of a relationship is ultimately a reflection of the resilience of love itself, as modeled by Christ's unconditional love for us.

PRACTICAL WISDOM NEEDED IN RELATIONSHIPS

i. Call for Help: Seeking Support in Relationships

Just as we don't hesitate to seek medical help when we sustain physical injuries, so too should we seek guidance and support when relationships face challenges. When we're hurt emotionally or relationally, trying to handle everything alone can lead to prolonged pain, confusion, and unresolved conflict. In Ecclesiastes 4:9-10 (NIV), it is written, *"Two are better than one, because they have a good return for their labor: If either of them falls down, one can help the other up."* This verse illustrates the wisdom in seeking help from others during times of difficulty. Relationships, whether in marriage, family, or friendships, require care and attention, and sometimes we need the support of others to navigate through tough times. Why should we endure isolation when God provides trusted people to offer counsel and support?

Seeking guidance and assistance is not a sign of weakness but an act of wisdom and humility. Proverbs 11:14 (NIV) states, *"For lack of guidance a nation falls, but victory is won through many advisers."* In the same way, the success and healing of our relationships require us to humble ourselves and seek the wisdom of those who can provide objective advice. Christian counselor Dr. John Townsend, co-author of *Boundaries*, emphasizes that "the quality of your relationships is determined by your willingness to seek help, to set limits, and to grow." Relationships grow and heal when we acknowledge that we cannot do everything alone. Are we open to receiving guidance when relationships begin to struggle, or do we pridefully try to handle things on our own?

The Bible also teaches us the importance of accountability and support within the community of believers. In Galatians 6:2 (NIV), Paul writes, *"Carry each other's burdens, and in this way you will fulfill the law of Christ."* Seeking help from trusted friends, mentors, or counselors isn't just about receiving advice, but about sharing the burden and allowing others to support us. Just as a physical injury can become more serious if ignored, relational issues can fester and grow if not addressed with the help of others. Are we willing to share our burdens with others, or do we prefer to carry them alone, even when we know it's too much?

Ultimately, seeking help in relationships is an act of trust in God's provision. In Proverbs 15:22 (NIV), it is written, "Plans fail for lack of counsel, but with many advisers they succeed." God has placed people in our lives to help us navigate difficult times, and when we seek their guidance, we align ourselves with His purpose for growth and healing. In the context of relationships, this means being vulnerable, asking for wisdom, and taking the necessary steps to restore unity. Do we trust that God has provided wise counsel in our lives, and are we willing to seek it when relationships face challenges? By reaching out for help, we demonstrate a commitment to healing, growth, and God's plan for our relational well-being.

ii. Invest in Healing:
The Time and Effort of Restoring Relationships

Healing in relationships, much like physical healing, requires time, effort, and intentional action. The process is not instantaneous; it requires patience and commitment to the journey of restoration. Just as a wound takes time to heal, emotional and relational wounds need time to mend, and often, it's a painful and slow process. The Bible speaks to this in Colossians 3:13 (NIV), where Paul encourages believers, *"Bear with each other and forgive one another if any of you has a grievance against someone. Forgive as the Lord forgave you."* Forgiveness is often the first step in healing, but it is not always easy or quick. It requires a heart willing to endure discomfort for the sake of reconciliation. Are we willing to commit to the slow and often painful process of healing relationships when they are broken?

Healing requires humility, the recognition that both parties in a relationship might have contributed to the fracture. It is tempting to hold on to pride or blame others, but true healing comes when we acknowledge our own shortcomings and sins. James 4:10 (NIV) says, *"Humble yourselves before the Lord, and he will lift you up."* When we humble ourselves before God, we are more inclined to humble ourselves before others, extending grace where there is conflict. Christian author and counselor, Gary Chapman, in his book The 5 Apologies of the Heart, writes, *"Forgiveness requires a humble heart, the ability to say, 'I was wrong,' and the courage to restore what was broken."* This humility opens the door for healing, not only for ourselves but for the other person as well. Have we set aside our pride long enough to see how healing can begin in our hearts and relationships?

Forgiveness is deeply intertwined with the investment required in healing relationships. It is not simply a matter of saying, "I forgive you," but a commitment to letting go of resentment and choosing to rebuild trust. In Matthew 18:21-22, Peter asks Jesus how many times he should forgive, and Jesus responds, *"I tell you, not seven times, but seventy-seven times."* This response underscores the continuous nature of forgiveness; it isn't a one-time event, but a process. Trust, once broken, takes time to rebuild. Christian author, C.S. Lewis, wisely states, *"To be a Christian means to forgive the inexcusable because God has forgiven the inexcusable in you."* Forgiveness is not easy, but it is necessary for healing. Do we truly understand the depth of forgiveness required in relationships, and are we willing to extend it even when it feels hard or unjust?

Therefore, investing in healing requires a deep willingness to rebuild the foundation of trust that has been damaged. Proverbs 16:3 (NIV) says, *"Commit to the Lord whatever you do, and he will establish your plans."* Healing is not something that we can accomplish on our own; it is a work that must be rooted in God's grace. As we seek God's guidance and strength, He provides the wisdom and patience needed to rebuild what has been broken. In the same way that a house is rebuilt with care and attention, relationships require intentional effort to restore them. As long as we are committed to God's plan for restoration and transformation, healing is possible. Are we willing to invest in the healing process, trusting that God will guide us in rebuilding what was lost and broken?

iii. Never Abandon What God Has Joined: The Sacredness of Relationships

Relationships, particularly marriage, are sacred in the eyes of God, and this truth is underscored throughout Scripture. Jesus Himself affirms this in Matthew 19:6 (NIV): *"So they are no longer two, but one flesh. Therefore what God has joined together, let no one separate."* This verse emphasizes the divine bond that exists within marriage. The commitment made before God in marriage is not just a contractual agreement but a covenant a deep, spiritual bond that should not be easily broken. In a world where divorce rates are high and relationships are often disposable, Christians are called to view marriage as sacred and enduring. Why, then, are we so quick to abandon relationships when challenges arise? Does not the Bible call us to honor what God has established and join together in His purpose for us?

Rather than giving up, believers are encouraged to focus on working through the pain and difficulties that inevitably arise in relationships. When facing marital struggles, it is easy to feel as if the situation is beyond repair. However, Scripture reminds us that God is the ultimate healer and restorer. In 1 Corinthians 13:7 (NIV), Paul writes, *"It always protects, always trusts, always hopes, always perseveres."* True love agape love is not a fleeting emotion but a decision to endure through trials and pain. When we are united in love, we are called to work through difficulties together, not give up at the first sign of hardship. As author Gary Chapman puts it in his book *The 5 Love Languages*, "In marriage, we need to look at our spouse's needs, not just our own. Marriage is about giving, not just receiving." Are we willing to focus on the mutual healing and growth necessary to preserve the sacred bond of marriage?

The choice to never abandon a relationship involves a commitment to enduring together, even in the most difficult of circumstances. The pain may feel unbearable at times, but it is through these moments that the relationship can grow stronger and more resilient. James 1:3-4 (NIV) encourages us, *"Because you know that the testing of your faith produces perseverance. Let perseverance finish its work so that you may be mature and complete, not lacking anything."* In this context, the struggles faced in a relationship can serve as opportunities for growth and maturity. Both partners are called to support and help each other through the hard times, relying on God for wisdom and strength. Christian author Tim Keller writes, *"Marriage is meant to be a picture of the gospel, and that is precisely why it requires such self-sacrifice."* In this light, should we view relationship struggles as opportunities for greater love and faithfulness?

Working through pain together, rather than abandoning what God has joined, requires a deep trust in God's sovereignty and wisdom. Romans 8:28 (NIV) assures us, *"And we know that in all things God works for the good of those who love him, who have been called according to his purpose."* Even in moments of pain, God is present, working in and through the relationship for His greater purposes. As we commit to preserving our relationships, we are called to trust that God will use the trials we face to strengthen and refine us. Relationships, especially marriage, are not about finding perfection, but about journeying together with God at the center. Are we willing to trust that God's design for our relationships is good, even in the midst of struggle?

PRIORITIZING LOVE OVER MATERIAL THINGS: THE ESSENCE OF TRUE RELATIONSHIPS

In relationships, true love transcends wealth, possessions, and outward success. The Bible consistently emphasizes the importance of love as the foundation of any meaningful relationship, especially when compared to material wealth. In 1 Corinthians 13:3 (NIV), Paul writes, *"If I give all I possess to the poor and give over my body to hardship that I may boast, but do not have love, I gain nothing."* This verse serves as a powerful reminder that love is the most valuable element in relationships. No amount of wealth, success, or material possessions can replace the depth and significance of genuine love and connection. In a society that often equates success with accumulation of wealth and status, we must ask ourselves: How much more meaningful would our relationships be if we focused more on the person rather than the possessions?

True love in relationships is evident in our willingness to be there for one another, especially during life's trials. In moments of difficulty, it's not the material things that offer comfort; it's the presence and emotional support of loved ones. Ecclesiastes 4:9-10 (NIV) speaks to this truth: *"Two are better than one, because they have a good return for their labor: If either of them falls down, one can help the other up. But pity anyone who falls and has no one to help them up."* In this passage, the value of companionship and mutual support in times of hardship is emphasized. Love, in its truest form, is shown through our willingness to be there for one another, offering help, encouragement, and presence. Does not the Bible remind us that material things will pass away, but love endures forever (1 Corinthians 13:8)?

The story of the woman who credited her dog for companionship in her final days offers a poignant illustration of this principle. The dog, unlike material possessions, did not offer wealth or external success. Instead, it provided unwavering loyalty, comfort, and presence. This mirrors the way love functions in human relationships. Love is not defined by what we can give materially but by how we show up for others when they need us most. As Christian author Tim Keller states in *The Meaning of Marriage*, *"Marriage is not about finding someone who will make you happy. It's about being willing to love and serve the other person, even when it's difficult."* Just as the dog in the story provided companionship without expecting anything in return, so should we offer unconditional love to others, especially in the hardest moments. How many times have we, as humans, missed the opportunity to show love because we were too focused on the material aspects of life?

Jesus Himself exemplifies this principle by prioritizing love and relationships over material wealth. In Matthew 6:19-21 (NIV), Jesus teaches, *"Do not store up for yourselves treasures on earth, where moths and vermin destroy, and where thieves break in and steal. But store up for yourselves treasures in heaven, where moths and vermin do not destroy, and where thieves do not break in and steal."* Jesus directs our focus to what truly matters our relationships with God and others. When we focus on love, loyalty, and mutual support, we are building eternal treasures that can never be taken away. As C.S. Lewis wisely noted, *"Love is not an emotion. It is a state of being that manifests itself through our actions."* In the end, will we find more joy in accumulating things, or will we cherish the love we share with those who are closest to us?

NAKEDNESS AS THE IDEAL RELATIONSHIP STATE

Nakedness, in its deepest sense, symbolizes openness and vulnerability, both essential for fostering authentic relationships. From a biblical perspective, nakedness is first introduced in Genesis 2:25: *"Adam and his wife were both naked, and they felt no shame."* This verse highlights the state of purity and transparency in the relationship between Adam and Eve before sin entered the world. It reflects an ideal where individuals can fully reveal themselves flaws, strengths, and all without fear of rejection or judgment. Can a relationship truly thrive if partners hide their true selves from each other? The act of being metaphorically "naked" allows people to connect on a profound level, where intimacy is not just physical but also emotional and spiritual.

Trust is the foundation that sustains the openness that nakedness demands. Without trust, the act of vulnerability becomes a risk rather than an opportunity for deeper connection. Proverbs 3:5 encourages believers to embrace trust, stating: *"Trust in the Lord with all your heart and lean not on your own understanding."* If trust in God forms the basis of one's life, then it can overflow into human relationships. How often do we allow fear and insecurity to prevent us from being truly open with those we love? As Christian author C.S. Lewis observed, *"To love at all is to be vulnerable."* Vulnerability requires a safe space where judgment is replaced by grace, reflecting the unconditional love God extends to humanity.

Nakedness in relationships also calls for mutual understanding and acceptance. True love acknowledges imperfections and chooses to embrace them. Colossians 3:13, NIV, reminds us: *"Bear with each other and forgive one another if any of you has a grievance against someone. Forgive as the Lord forgave you."* Acceptance is not about ignoring flaws but about recognizing the beauty of imperfection and supporting growth.

How can couples nurture an atmosphere of acceptance if they focus only on each other's faults? In his book *The Four Loves*, C.S. Lewis emphasizes, *"Love is not affectionate feeling, but a steady wish for the loved person's ultimate good as far as it can be obtained."* This perspective aligns with the mutual commitment that nakedness in relationships demands.

Nakedness also holds a spiritual significance, reminding us of God's desire for a transparent relationship with His children. Hebrews 4:13, NIV, declares: *"Nothing in all creation is hidden from God's sight. Everything is uncovered and laid bare before the eyes of him to whom we must give account."* Just as God invites us to approach Him with honesty and humility, relationships flourish when both parties mirror this spiritual nakedness. Are we willing to lay down our masks and reveal our true selves, trusting in grace to cover us? In *Sacred Marriage*, Gary Thomas writes, "Marriage is a journey toward holiness, not just happiness." Similarly, the nakedness within relationships represents a pursuit of deeper spiritual unity, aligning human connections with divine purpose. By embracing the metaphorical nakedness of openness, trust, mutual understanding, and spiritual vulnerability, relationships can mirror the divine example of love and transparency shown by God Himself.

THE POWER OF HUMAN CONNECTION AND SPIRITUAL NAKEDNESS

The power of human connection and spiritual nakedness lies in the profound truth that our greatest need is not material wealth or status but genuine relationships. Nakedness, both literal and symbolic, represents the essence of authentic living by being open, honest, and vulnerable. Genesis 2:25, NIV, beautifully captures this state of innocence and unity: *"Adam and his wife were both naked, and they felt no shame."* This image reveals that true fulfilment comes not from what we possess but from how deeply we connect with others. What would relationships look like if we let go of the walls we build to shield ourselves? As Dietrich Bonhoeffer wrote in *Life Together*, "The person who loves their dream of community will destroy community, but the person who loves those around them will create community." This love thrives in the naked honesty of connection.

Spiritual nakedness in relationships requires a bold surrender of pretense and self-reliance. It involves letting go of the masks we wear to impress others, allowing our true selves to emerge. Paul's words in 2 Corinthians 12:9, NIV, remind us of the beauty in vulnerability: *"But he said to me, 'My grace is sufficient for you, for my power is made perfect in weakness.'"* When we admit our flaws and struggles, we open the door for God's grace to transform us and our relationships. Can we trust others with our weaknesses, just as God trusts us to steward His grace? Christian writer Henri Nouwen noted, *"The friend who can be silent with us in a moment of despair or confusion, who can stay with us in an hour of grief and bereavement, who can tolerate not knowing...that is a friend who cares."*

True intimacy and unity are born when we embrace the nakedness of mutual trust and vulnerability. Relationships grounded in spiritual openness are not transactional; they are transformative. Ephesians 4:2-3, NIV, urges believers to foster such relationships: *"Be completely humble and gentle; be patient, bearing with one another in love. Make every effort to keep the unity of the Spirit through the bond of peace."* Nakedness in this sense is not about exposing weaknesses to exploit them but about creating a safe space for love to flourish. How often do we prioritize appearances or accomplishments over authentic connection? Gary Chapman, in *The Five Love Languages*, writes, "Love is a choice you make every day." Nakedness in love is a daily decision to honor and cherish the vulnerability of others.

Hence, spiritual nakedness is a testament to our trust in God's sovereignty over our relationships. Hebrews 4:13, NIV, says, *"Nothing in all creation is hidden from God's sight. Everything is uncovered and laid bare before the eyes of him to whom we must give account."* This divine nakedness inspires us to live authentically, knowing that God sees and loves us entirely. Are we willing to extend the same grace and transparency to others? As C.S. Lewis reflected in *Mere Christianity*, "To love is to be vulnerable." In embracing the nakedness of human connection, we mirror God's design for relationships a reflection of His love and a pathway to true fulfillment.

NOTE THESE

Love is more valuable than material wealth: True relationships thrive on love, not possessions or success.

Genuine love is shown through presence and support: Being there for others in difficult times matters more than material gifts.

Openness and vulnerability strengthen relationships: Trust and transparency foster deeper connections.

True love accepts flaws and encourages growth: Relationships flourish when partners embrace each other's imperfections.

Spiritual connection is essential in relationships: Love mirrors God's unconditional love, prioritizing eternal treasures over temporary wealth.

CHAPTER THIRTEEN

GOD AT THE CENTER: THE KEY TO GENUINE CONNECTION

God at the center of our lives and relationships is the cornerstone of genuine connection and true fulfilment. Yet, many families and relationships today operate on human wisdom, traditions, and self-reliance, leaving little room for God's transformative presence. This often leads to instability, as human wisdom is inherently limited. Proverbs 3:5-6, NIV, offers a clear directive: *"Trust in the Lord with all your heart and lean not on your own understanding; in all your ways submit to him, and he will make your paths straight."* How often do we trust our plans over God's wisdom, only to find ourselves in turmoil? Spiritual nakedness, in this context, is about surrendering control to God and acknowledging that He alone can provide the guidance we need for thriving relationships. As Tozer aptly noted, "The reason why many are still troubled, still seeking, still making little forward progress is because they haven't come to the end of themselves yet."

God's invitation to deep connection is vividly expressed in Revelation 3:20, NIV, *"Here I am! I stand at the door and knock. If anyone hears my voice and opens the door, I will come in and eat with that person, and they with me."* This verse underscores God's desire for intimate fellowship with us, an invitation that extends to our relationships with others. When

God is at the center, He becomes the unifying force that fosters love, patience, and understanding. Can we truly expect lasting connections without anchoring them in the one who created love itself? In *The Meaning of Marriage*, Timothy Keller emphasizes, *"If God is not at the center of your marriage, it is just two people trying to get from each other the deep need for love that only God can fill."*

Spiritual nakedness in relationships is an acknowledgement of our dependence on God. It means recognizing our limitations and allowing God's wisdom and grace to guide our actions. This humility opens the door for His presence to shape every aspect of our lives. Matthew 6:33, NIV, reminds us: *"But seek first his kingdom and his righteousness, and all these things will be given to you as well."* How often do we prioritize personal desires over seeking God's will? In doing so, we hinder the flow of His blessings. As Oswald Chambers wrote in *My Utmost for His Highest*, "When we no longer seek God for His blessings, but for Himself, we find that all we ever wanted is in Him."

God's presence is the key to creating space for authenticity and connection. When we invite Him into our hearts and relationships, we move beyond superficial bonds to build connections rooted in grace and truth. This level of spiritual nakedness allows us to extend the same grace to others that God has shown us. Philippians 4:13, NIV, assures us: *"I can do all this through him who gives me strength."* Are we willing to admit our need for His strength and surrender our self-reliance? When we do, we not only honor God but also cultivate relationships that reflect His love and glory, fulfilling His purpose for our lives.

SPIRITUAL NAKEDNESS: HUMILITY AND VULNERABILITY

Spiritual nakedness, rooted in humility and vulnerability, is a profound lesson in recognizing our dependence on God rather than leaning on our limited human understanding. Often, we project an image of self-sufficiency in relationships, as if we can navigate challenges and decisions alone. Yet, Proverbs 3:5-6, NIV, warns: *"Trust in the Lord with all your heart and lean not on your own understanding; in all your ways submit to him, and he will make your paths straight."* This scripture reminds us that surrendering control to God is not a sign of weakness but a necessary act of wisdom. Why do we hesitate to admit our need for divine guidance, knowing that God's understanding far surpasses ours? Spiritual nakedness, in this sense, requires a stripping away of pride and an openness to God's direction, teaching current and future generations that humility is the foundation of a life and relationships aligned with His purpose.

The imagery of Adam and Eve being naked before God and each other, as described in Genesis 2:25, NIV, *"Adam and his wife were both naked, and they felt no shame"* serves as a model for spiritual vulnerability. This state of openness signifies a relationship free from fear and full of trust, both with God and with one another. In contemporary relationships, particularly in marriage, spiritual nakedness translates into practices such as praying together, sharing burdens, and seeking God's wisdom during conflicts. How often do couples rely solely on human reasoning to resolve disputes, neglecting the power of prayer and divine intervention? Christian author Gary Thomas, in *Sacred Marriage*, observes, "What if God designed marriage to make us holy more than to make us happy?" This perspective encourages couples to view humility and vulnerability not as obstacles but as pathways to a deeper, God-centered connection.

For current and future generations, embracing spiritual nakedness means acknowledging that relationships thrive not through self-reliance but through divine reliance. The act of surrendering control allows God's wisdom to guide our choices, fostering unity and understanding. In Ephesians 4:2-3, NIV, Paul advises: *"Be completely humble and gentle; be patient, bearing with one another in love. Make every effort to keep the unity of the Spirit through the bond of peace."* This humility, reflected in spiritual nakedness, equips us to prioritize God's will over personal pride, teaching others the value of leaning on God's strength. How can we expect lasting peace and unity without first submitting to the one who is the source of both? In his book *The Meaning of Marriage*,

Timothy Keller emphasizes, "To be loved but not known is comforting but superficial. To be known and not loved is our greatest fear. But to be fully known and truly loved is, well, a lot like being loved by God."

Spiritual nakedness, as a legacy for future generations, teaches that humility and vulnerability are not signs of weakness but marks of spiritual maturity. By surrendering control to God, we model a dependence on His wisdom that transcends fleeting human knowledge. Philippians 4:13, NIV, reassures us: *"I can do all this through him who gives me strength."* This truth inspires individuals, families, and communities to trust God fully, fostering relationships built on His unshakable foundation. Will we continue to rely on ourselves, or will we demonstrate to those who come after us that true strength lies in humility and vulnerability before God? By embracing spiritual nakedness, we pass down a legacy of faith, trust, and God-centered living that transforms relationships and enriches lives for generations to come.

CHRIST'S LOVE AND THE SYMBOLISM OF NAKEDNESS IN MARRIAGE

Christ's love, as symbolized by nakedness in marriage, offers a profound picture of intimacy, vulnerability, and connection between Christ and His Church. The Song of Solomon 5:1-2, NIV, reflects this deep union: *"I have come into my garden, my sister, my bride; I have gathered my myrrh with my spice. I have eaten my honeycomb and my honey; I have drunk my wine and my milk."* The imagery of honeycomb, wine, and milk represents the spiritual nourishment of God's Word, the sweetness of His promises, and the joy of His Spirit. This relationship invites believers to a closeness with Christ that transcends mere ritual or obligation. Just as the beloved in the Song declares, *"I sleep, but my heart is awake,"* we are reminded that Christ continually longs for a connection with us. Are we truly awake to His call, or do the distractions of life cause us to miss the intimacy He offers?

This invitation to intimacy is echoed in Revelation 3:20, NIV: *"Here I am! I stand at the door and knock. If anyone hears my voice and opens the door, I will come in and eat with that person, and they with me."* The imagery of Christ knocking reflects His desire for a relationship built on mutual openness and love. In marriage, this is paralleled by a couple's spiritual nakedness laying aside pride, fear, and self-reliance to create a bond where God's presence is central. How often do we approach relationships guarded, unwilling to fully trust? C.S. Lewis captures this beautifully in *The Four Loves*: "To love at all is to be vulnerable. Love anything, and your heart will certainly be wrung and possibly broken." Vulnerability, whether with God or a spouse, requires courage but yields the deepest connection.

For current and future generations, the lesson here is clear: authentic relationships thrive when God is at the center. In marriage, spiritual nakedness allows God's love to flow freely, strengthening the bond between husband and wife. Ephesians 5:25-27, NIV, offers guidance: *"Husbands, love your wives, just as Christ loved the church and gave himself up for her to make her holy, cleansing her by the washing with water through the word, and to present her to himself as a radiant church, without stain or wrinkle or any other blemish."* This love is sacrificial and purifying, mirroring the divine love Christ has for His Church. How can future generations learn to prioritize selflessness in relationships without this example of Christ-like love?

So, embracing Christ's love and the symbolism of nakedness in marriage teaches us to live lives of transparency, humility, and trust. This vulnerability is not a weakness but the strength to allow God's transformative power to work through us. As Timothy Keller writes in *The Meaning of Marriage*, "To be fully loved but not fully known is comforting but superficial. To be fully known and truly loved is a lot like being loved by God." By modeling this love in our relationships, we leave a legacy of faith and authenticity for future generations, showing that God's love is the foundation of all meaningful connections. Are we prepared to let go of our fears and embrace the fullness of Christ's love in our lives and relationships? This willingness not only shapes us but also sets an example of godly love for those who follow.

NAKEDNESS AS SURRENDER: LETTING GOD LEAD

Nakedness as surrender symbolizes a profound act of yielding our lives to God's sovereignty. In the Garden of Eden, Adam and Eve existed in perfect unity with God, naked and unashamed, as seen in Genesis 2:25 (NLT): *"Now the man and his wife were both naked, but they felt no shame."* This nakedness reflected a state of innocence, openness, and dependence on God. However, when sin entered, they covered themselves and hid, as described in Genesis 3:10 (NLT): *"I heard you walking in the garden, so I hid. I was afraid because I was naked."* Their shame and fear illustrate humanity's instinct to conceal flaws and mistakes rather than trust God's love and forgiveness. Isn't it true that even today, we often hide from God, reluctant to admit our struggles? Spiritual nakedness invites us back to that original state of surrender, where we no longer rely on our abilities but trust God completely.

This surrender is essential not only for our personal walk with God but also in our relationships. Proverbs 3:5-6 (NLT) reminds us: *"Trust in the Lord with all your heart; do not depend on your own understanding. Seek his will in all you do, and he will show you which path to take."* When we let go of the need to control every situation and allow God to lead, we find clarity and strength to navigate life's complexities. How often do we exhaust ourselves trying to solve problems that only God can handle? As A.W. Tozer wrote in *The Pursuit of God*, "The man who has God for his treasure has all things in One." This truth emphasizes that surrendering to God not only aligns us with His will but also fulfils our deepest needs.

For marriages and relationships, surrendering to God's guidance creates a foundation of trust and mutual support. It allows couples to seek God's wisdom together, fostering unity and resilience in times of conflict or uncertainty. Ephesians 5:21 (NLT) says, *"And further, submit to one another out of reverence for Christ."* This mutual submission reflects the spiritual nakedness of surrender, where both partners prioritize God's will over personal pride or agendas. Isn't it in our vulnerability before God that we find strength in each other? As Gary Thomas noted in *Sacred Marriage*, "What if God designed marriage to make us holy more than to make us happy?" Surrendering to God shapes us into better partners, teaching us humility, patience, and sacrificial love.

For current and future generations, the lesson is clear: true strength lies in surrendering to God. This act of spiritual nakedness teaches us to trust Him in every aspect of life, allowing His wisdom to guide our decisions and His love to heal our brokenness. Philippians 4:13 (NLT) reminds us, *"For I can do everything through Christ, who gives me strength."* Are we willing to trust God with every area of our lives, including our relationships, careers, and dreams? By modeling this surrender, we leave a legacy of faith and dependence on God, showing future generations that success and fulfillment are found not in self-reliance but in complete reliance on Him. Through spiritual nakedness, we invite God to transform us, equipping us to face life's challenges with grace and confidence in His unfailing love.

TRUE CONNECTION THROUGH SPIRITUAL NAKEDNESS

True connection through spiritual nakedness begins with the willingness to approach relationships with openness, vulnerability, and dependence on God. In Genesis 2:25 (NLT), we read, *"Now the man and his wife were both naked, but they felt no shame."* This verse captures the essence of God's design for relationships: transparency without fear or pretense. Spiritual nakedness reflects this ideal, urging us to lay down the masks we often wear and to trust God fully as we engage with others. Isn't it true that hiding our true selves often creates distance rather than closeness? By returning to this state of spiritual openness, we allow God to heal and transform our relationships, anchoring them in His grace and truth.

God's presence is essential for deep, meaningful connections. Proverbs 16:3 (NLT) reminds us, *"Commit your actions to the Lord, and your plans will succeed."* When we invite God into our relationships, whether in marriage, friendship, or family, He becomes the foundation upon which true intimacy is built. How often do we attempt to strengthen our relationships without first seeking God's guidance? As Dietrich Bonhoeffer wrote in *Life Together*, "Only in Jesus Christ are we one; only through Him are we bound together." This unity transcends human effort as God's love flows through us, enabling us to connect on a deeper level with those around us.

Spiritual nakedness requires surrendering control and trusting God to guide our interactions. In 2 Corinthians 12:9 (NLT), Paul recounts God's words: *"My grace is all you need. My power works best in weakness."* Vulnerability is not a sign of weakness but a pathway to experiencing God's strength. In relationships, this means being honest about our struggles and fears, allowing God to work through our imperfections. Isn't it in moments of openness that we experience the most profound connection? As Henri Nouwen stated in *The Wounded Healer*, "When we become aware that we do not have to escape our pains but can mobilize them into a common search for life, those very pains are transformed from expressions of despair into signs of hope."

For current and future generations, this principle serves as a powerful lesson: true connection is found not in perfection or self-reliance but in authenticity and dependence on God. By modeling spiritual nakedness in our relationships, we demonstrate the beauty of trusting God and each other with our vulnerabilities. James 5:16 (NLT) encourages us: *"Confess your sins to each other and pray for each other so that you may be healed."* Are we willing to embrace this level of openness, trusting God to strengthen our relationships? By doing so, we create a legacy of love and grace, showing future generations that God's presence is the key to lasting, fulfilling connections. Through spiritual nakedness, we reflect God's love, inviting others to experience the divine intimacy He desires for all His children.

NAKEDNESS AND THE INTIMATE RELATIONSHIP CHRIST DESIRES WITH US

Nakedness in the Bible represent an invitation to humility, purity, and unfiltered openness before God. In the Song of Solomon 5:2 (NLT), we read, *"I slept, but my heart was awake, when I heard my lover knocking and calling: 'Open to me, my treasure, my darling, my dove, my perfect one.'"* This imagery symbolizes the intimate relationship Christ desires with us, one where vulnerability is met with unwavering love. The dew on His head and the drops of the night signify Christ's persistence and humility in pursuing us, even when we hesitate to open our hearts. Isn't it humbling to think that the King of kings patiently waits for us to respond to His love?

Imagine a king stepping into a modest home, not with pomp and ceremony but with the humility of a traveler seeking refuge. This reflects Christ's approach to our hearts: not with demands but with a gentle invitation. Revelation 3:20 (NLT) reinforces this imagery: *"Look! I stand at the door and knock. If you hear my voice and open the door, I will come in, and we will share a meal together as friends."* Christ, the sovereign Creator, desires a relationship based on mutual trust and openness, free of pretense. How often do we hold back from Him, clinging to pride or fear, rather than embracing the intimacy He offers? As Charles Spurgeon eloquently said, "He stands at the door, not because He is shut out by us, but because He desires to come in to bless."

This spiritual nakedness invites us to meet Christ with the same humility and transparency He shows us. It means shedding the layers of pride, self-sufficiency, and hidden sin that separate us from Him. Hebrews 4:13 (NLT) reminds us, *"Nothing in all creation is hidden from God. Everything is naked and exposed before His eyes, and He is the one to whom we are accountable."* When we come before Christ with nothing to hide, we experience His love in its fullness—a love that heals, restores, and transforms. Can we truly experience intimacy with Christ if we are unwilling to be vulnerable? Dietrich Bonhoeffer captured this truth well when he wrote, "Being a Christian is less about cautiously avoiding sin than about courageously and actively doing God's will."

For future generations, this lesson is invaluable: true intimacy with Christ begins with spiritual nakedness. By modeling this openness in our relationship with God, we teach others to trust in His grace and approach Him without fear. This transparency not only strengthens our bond with Christ but also encourages authentic relationships with others, rooted in love and humility. Philippians 2:7-8 (NLT) illustrates Christ's example: *"Instead, He gave up His divine privileges; He took the humble position of a slave and was born as a human being. When He appeared in human form, He humbled Himself in obedience to God and died a criminal's death on a cross."* Are we willing to follow His example of vulnerability and surrender? By doing so, we leave a legacy of faith that shows future generations the beauty of an intimate relationship with Christ, a relationship that begins with the courage to stand spiritually naked before Him.

NOTE THESE

True connection begins with openness and vulnerability: Spiritual nakedness invites us to approach relationships without pretense, trusting God fully.

God's presence is key to meaningful relationships: Inviting God into our relationships creates a foundation for true intimacy.

Vulnerability leads to God's strength: Embracing our imperfections allows God's grace to transform our relationships.

Authenticity and dependence on God foster lasting connections: True connection is built on transparency and trust in God's guidance.

Spiritual nakedness deepens intimacy with Christ: Embracing humility and vulnerability with God leads to deeper spiritual closeness and transformation.

CHAPTER FOURTEEN

The Challenge of Spiritual Openness

The challenge of spiritual openness is deeply rooted in the tension between the desire for intimacy with God and the distractions of our daily lives. In Song of Solomon 5:2 (NLT), the beloved says, *"I slept, but my heart was awake. When I heard my lover knocking, I jumped up to open to my lover."* This verse paints a picture of the struggle many face in trying to respond to God's call amidst the noise and busyness of life. How often do we hear God calling us, yet find ourselves too preoccupied with the distractions of the world to fully open our hearts to Him? The call to spiritual intimacy requires us to be intentional, creating space in our lives for God's presence. We must ask ourselves: are we truly listening when God knocks at the door of our hearts, or are we too caught up in our own pursuits?

Nakedness, it's about clearing away distractions and preparing our hearts to receive God's love. Just as the practice of foot washing was an act of cleansing, we must also cleanse our hearts to be ready for deeper communion with God. In John 13:8 (NLT), Jesus tells Peter, *"Unless I wash you, you won't belong to me."* This statement speaks to the necessity of purification before entering into spiritual closeness with Christ. The distractions of life often muddy our spiritual vision, making it difficult to see God clearly. What would happen if we took time daily to "wash" our hearts of distractions, sin, and the burdens that weigh us down?

Spiritual openness requires humility and a willingness to surrender to God's cleansing power. Just as the disciples needed their feet washed before entering into a new phase of spiritual understanding, we too must be willing to allow God to cleanse our hearts before we can enter into the fullness of His presence. In James 4:8 (NLT), we are called to *"Come close to God, and God will come close to you. Wash your hands, you sinners; purify your hearts, for your loyalty is divided between God and the world."* This call to repentance and spiritual preparation is essential for a deeper relationship with God. How often do we try to approach God without first cleansing our hearts of the distractions that hinder our intimacy with Him? This verse serves as a reminder that spiritual openness requires us to examine our hearts and take action to clear the path for God's presence.

For us to fully embrace spiritual intimacy, we must commit to the discipline of repentance and prayer. By doing so, we allow God to renew us, purify us, and make us ready to experience the depth of His love. The Song of Solomon, with its imagery of the beloved's longing for intimacy, reflects the desire God has for us to experience a deeper relationship with Him. When we clear away distractions, humble ourselves, and invite God into our hearts, we are preparing ourselves for the full measure of His love. In this way, we find that nakedness, in the spiritual sense, becomes a symbol of readiness ready to be filled with God's love and presence. Now, let's delve into the following challenges below;

i. Distractions of the World

One of the greatest challenges to spiritual openness is the constant barrage of distractions in our lives. From social media to work pressures, the world constantly competes for our attention. In Matthew 13:22 (NLT), Jesus warns, *"The seed that fell among the thorns represents those* who hear God's word, but all too quickly the message is crowded out by the worries of this life and the lure of wealth, so no fruit is produced." The world's distractions can stifle our ability to hear God's voice and respond to His call. The secular worldview often emphasizes success, materialism, and individual achievement, which can leave little room for spiritual growth.

ii. Pride and Self-Reliance

Spiritual openness requires humility, but pride and self-reliance often create barriers. Proverbs 3:5-6 (NLT) encourages us, *"Trust in the Lord with all your heart; do not depend on your own understanding. Seek His will in all you do, and He will show you which path to take."* The temptation to rely on our own wisdom can hinder our ability to fully surrender to God. The world's emphasis on self-sufficiency and individualism can make it difficult to acknowledge our need for God's guidance and grace.

iii. Fear of Vulnerability:

Spiritual nakedness involves exposing our true selves to God, but many fear being vulnerable. In 1 John 4:18 (NLT), we are reminded, *"Such love has no fear because perfect love expels all fear."* Fear of rejection or shame can keep us from opening up to God and others. The culture often teaches us to hide our weaknesses and flaws, creating a barrier to authentic spiritual connection.

iv. Lack of Spiritual Discipline

Spiritual openness requires ongoing discipline, such as prayer, repentance, and studying God's Word. In Matthew 26:41 (NLT), Jesus tells His disciples, *"Keep watch and pray, so that you will not give in to temptation. For the spirit is willing, but the body is weak."* The lack of consistent spiritual practices can hinder our growth and openness to God. The modern world's fast-paced lifestyle often deprioritizes spiritual disciplines, making it difficult to maintain a close relationship with God.

v. *Division Between God and the World*

James 4:4 (NLT) warns, *"You adulterers! Don't you realize that friendship with the world makes you an enemy of God? I say it again: If you want to be a friend of the world, you make yourself an enemy of God."* Spiritual openness requires a clear choice to prioritize God above all else. The world's values often conflict with God's values, and this division can create a barrier to full intimacy with God. Modern society's acceptance of materialism, pleasure-seeking, and secularism can lead us to compromise our spiritual integrity and hinder our ability to experience the fullness of God's love.

In overcoming these challenges, we are encouraged to turn away from the distractions and temptations of the world, humbly seek God's guidance, and embrace spiritual vulnerability. This practice serves as a vital lesson for current and future generations: true spiritual intimacy and openness with God require intentionality, humility, and a willingness to surrender to His will. By addressing these challenges, we can create a more authentic relationship with God and experience the depth of His love and grace.

THE FLEETING NATURE OF SPIRITUAL OPPORTUNITY

In the Song of Solomon, the beloved expresses deep sorrow upon discovering that her lover has left after she had taken her time to prepare herself. This moment is symbolic of the fleeting nature of spiritual opportunity. In Song of Solomon 5:6 (NLT), she laments, *"When I opened to my lover, he was gone. My heart sank. I searched for him but could not find him. I called to him, but there was no reply."* This passage illustrates that God's call is not always guaranteed to be present. While Christ knocks at the door of our hearts, we must respond without delay. How often do we delay our response to God's invitation, thinking that He will always be there waiting? The beloved's experience serves as a stark reminder that we should not take God's call for granted, as the opportunity to embrace His love and guidance may pass us by if we are not vigilant and responsive.

Spiritual nakedness in this context symbolizes urgency and readiness. It's not just about being vulnerable but about being fully aware of God's presence in our lives and responding to Him without hesitation. Revelation 3:20 (NLT) says, *"Look! I stand at the door and knock. If you hear my voice and open the door, I will come in, and we will share a meal together as friends."* The imagery of Christ knocking on the door of our hearts represents an invitation to intimacy, but that invitation requires a timely response. If we delay or ignore God's call, we risk missing the opportunity for a deeper relationship with Him. Are we prepared to answer His call the moment He knocks, or do we allow distractions and the busyness of life to drown out His voice?

The sorrow the beloved feels when she misses her opportunity is a powerful metaphor for the regret that follows spiritual neglect. In 2 Corinthians 6:2 (NLT), Paul reminds us, *"For God says, 'At just the right time, I heard you. On the day of salvation, I helped you.' Indeed, the 'right time' is now. Today is the day of salvation."* This verse emphasizes the urgency of responding to God's invitation. Just as the beloved misses the moment to be with her lover, we too can miss the moment of spiritual awakening if we are not sensitive to God's timing. The urgency to act when God calls is not just a call for individual salvation but also a call to live a life of constant awareness, where we always remain spiritually alert and receptive to His voice.

In a world that is constantly moving at a fast pace, it's easy to overlook spiritual opportunities. The pressures of daily life, career ambitions, and personal distractions often take precedence over spiritual matters. However, the Bible teaches us to live in a state of readiness, as seen in Matthew 25:13 (NLT), where Jesus warns, *"So you, too, must keep watch! For you do not know the day or hour of my return."* This call to vigilance serves as a reminder that spiritual opportunities are fleeting, and we must be ready to respond when God calls. For current and future generations, this is a crucial lesson: to prioritize spiritual awareness over worldly distractions and to recognize that God's timing is always perfect. The delay in responding to His call may not only result in missed opportunities but also in spiritual stagnation. As we cultivate a lifestyle of readiness and attentiveness, we can embrace the fullness of God's love and direction, ensuring that we do not let the fleeting nature of spiritual opportunity slip away.

EMBRACING VULNERABILITY: THE PATH TO PURITY AND TRANSPARENCY WITH GOD

In God's eyes, nakedness is much more than a physical state; it symbolizes purity, honesty, and faithfulness. From the beginning, God created man and woman naked, not just physically but in a spiritual sense, representing a state of perfect communion with Him. In Genesis 2:25 (NLT), it says, *"Now the man and his wife were both naked, but they felt no shame."* This moment is pivotal because it highlights that there was nothing between them and God, and nothing was hidden. The absence of shame indicates a pure relationship where vulnerability was embraced, not feared. Just as Adam and Eve were unashamed in their nakedness before God, we too are called to stand before Him with complete openness, allowing His light to expose and cleanse us. In our walk with God, can we truly say we are transparent before Him, or do we hide parts of ourselves, hoping He won't notice our flaws?

Spiritual nakedness goes beyond mere vulnerability; it represents complete surrender and openness to God's will. When we stand before God with no barriers no masks, no pretenses—we are acknowledging our dependence on Him. As seen in Psalm 51:17 (NLT), *"The sacrifice you desire is a broken spirit. You will not reject a broken and repentant heart, O God."* This verse emphasizes that God desires a heart that is willing to admit its flaws and seek His forgiveness. Spiritual nakedness means being honest about our shortcomings, acknowledging our need for His grace, and allowing His love to fill the spaces where pride once resided. Are we willing to be spiritually vulnerable before God, knowing that He is both our Creator and our Redeemer, offering forgiveness and healing?

This openness is not just about admitting our flaws to God but also extends to our relationships with others. In a marriage, for example, spiritual nakedness can manifest as open communication, where both partners share their fears, hopes, and struggles without fear of judgment. Ephesians 5:21-25 (NLT) speaks of mutual submission in marriage, where husbands and wives are called to submit to one another out of reverence for Christ. The concept of transparency in this context is vital because it creates a bond of trust and intimacy. If one partner hides their struggles or feelings out of fear or shame, it creates walls that hinder growth and intimacy. In any relationship, spiritual nakedness allows both parties to rely on God for healing, guidance, and restoration. What happens when we refuse to share our true selves in relationships? Do we miss out on the intimacy and trust that God desires for us?

Spiritual nakedness ultimately calls for purity of heart, a state where our connection to God is prioritized above all else. In John 15:5 (NLT), Jesus says, *"Yes, I am the vine; you are the branches. Those who remain in me, and I in them, will produce much fruit. For apart from me you can do nothing."* This verse underlines the necessity of staying connected to God in all aspects of our lives. Just as a vine and branches share an inseparable connection, our relationship with God must be transparent, honest, and pure. When we remove the barriers of pride, fear, and shame, we allow God's presence to work in us, making us more like Him. This message serves as a lesson for both current and future generations to cultivate relationships that are founded on transparency, honesty, and a deep reliance on God. In a world that often values self-sufficiency and perfection, embracing spiritual nakedness is an act of humility and faith. It is through this vulnerability that we can experience the fullness of God's love and grace. How can we expect to grow in our relationship with God if we continue to hide parts of ourselves from Him?

UNITY IN GOD'S PURPOSE: EMBRACING SPIRITUAL NAKEDNESS FOR TRUE CONNECTION

The power of unity in God's will is evident from the very beginning of creation, where Adam and Eve were placed in a state of spiritual and physical nakedness, symbolizing complete openness and unity with each other and with God. Genesis 2:25 (NLT) says, *"Now the man and his wife were both naked, but they felt no shame."* This passage highlights the purity of their relationship, where there was no separation between them and God. Their unity was not just a physical bond but a spiritual one, reflecting God's intention for humanity to live in harmony with one another and with Him. In this original state of unity, they were in perfect alignment with God's will. How many times do we allow distractions, sin, or pride to divide us from this perfect unity? Are we striving to maintain the purity of unity that God originally intended for us?

Spiritual nakedness is not just about exposing our vulnerabilities; it is about aligning our hearts, minds, and actions with God's will. In Romans 12:2 (NLT), Paul urges us, *"Don't copy the behavior and customs of this world, but let God transform you into a new person by changing the way you think. Then you will learn to know God's will for you, which is good and pleasing and perfect."* This transformation is a result of spiritual nakedness allowing God to shape us, removing the distractions and personal agendas that prevent us from fully surrendering to His will. By being spiritually open, we are inviting God to mold us into His image, reflecting His love, grace, and purpose in our lives. What would it look like if we all fully surrendered to God's will? Could we achieve the unity and peace that He desires for us?

When we walk in the unity of God's will, we are also walking in the fullness of His purpose for our lives. This does not mean that our lives will be free from challenges, but rather that we are equipped with God's wisdom and guidance to navigate them. Ephesians 4:3-6 (NLT) urges us to *"Make every effort to keep yourselves united in the*

Spirit, binding yourselves together with peace. For there is one body and one Spirit, just as you have been called to one glorious hope for the future. There is one Lord, one faith, one baptism, one God and Father of all, who is over all, in all, and living through all." These verses emphasize that unity is a personal pursuit and a collective one God's will is for His people to walk together in harmony, reflecting the unity that exists within the Godhead. How often do we let division, whether in our families, churches, or communities, disrupt the unity that God desires? Are we truly making every effort to live in peace and unity with one another?

The power of unity in God's will is an essential lesson for both current and future generations. In a world marked by division, competition, and self-interest, the call to spiritual nakedness being fully surrendered to God's will offers a powerful antidote. When we choose unity over division, humility over pride, and surrender over self-will, we create an environment where God's love can thrive. As Christian author Dietrich Bonhoeffer said, *"The more we grow in God, the more we come to recognize that our greatest joy comes from being a part of His body, united with other believers in love and truth."* This unity is not just about agreement, but about walking in God's purpose together, fulfilling His plan for humanity. The lesson for future generations is clear: unity in God's will is not optional but essential for a life that reflects His love and advances His Kingdom.

SPIRITUAL NAKEDNESS AS THE KEY TO RELATIONSHIP AND LIFE SUCCESS

Spiritual nakedness is more than just a metaphor; it represents the humility and vulnerability we must embrace in all our relationships, whether with God or with others. In the context of marriage, family, and friendships, being spiritually naked means approaching each relationship with a heart willing to be open, transparent, and pure before God. It is a life of surrendering to His guidance and allowing His love to heal and shape us. We are not talking about worldly exposure, but rather the willingness to be vulnerable in our faith, knowing that

God can cleanse our hearts and direct our steps. As we open ourselves up to God and each other, we create space for the kind of connection that transcends superficiality, aligning our lives with God's will. We ask ourselves: How can we expect to build meaningful relationships if we are not first open to the Creator of those relationships? When we let go of control and allow God to lead us, our lives begin to flow according to His purpose, and this transforms not just our relationships but the way we approach every aspect of life.

The Bible offers deep lessons on the importance of spiritual nakedness. For instance, in John 13:5 (NLT), we see Jesus washing His disciples' feet, a powerful symbol of humility and vulnerability: *"Then he poured water into a basin and began to wash his disciples' feet, drying them with the towel that was wrapped around him."* This act demonstrated the importance of humility in relationships with Jesus, Though Jesus was their Teacher and Lord, He chose to humble Himself in service to His disciples. Similarly, in the Song of Solomon, the longing for intimacy between the lover and the beloved speaks to the deep desire for connection, which can only be realized when both parties are willing to be open and vulnerable. We can reflect on this question: Are we too proud or self-sufficient to open ourselves to the cleansing and guidance of God in our relationships? The lessons from these biblical examples remind us that the key to success in life and relationships is vulnerability, humility, and surrender to God's will. It is when we are spiritually naked before Him, laying down our own agendas, that we allow His presence to transform us and our relationships.

The concept of spiritual nakedness is also deeply rooted in the original relationship between Adam and Eve in the Garden of Eden. Genesis 2:25 (NLT) tells us, *"Now the man and his wife were both naked, but they felt no shame."* Before sin entered the world, they were completely transparent, not only with each other but with God. This reflects the ideal relationship God desires for us to be open and unashamed in His presence. The fall of humanity in Genesis 3, when Adam and Eve hid from God after sinning, serves as a powerful reminder that shame and pride block our connection with God and each other. In today's world, many people hide their vulnerabilities, wear masks, or rely on their own understanding, thinking that self-sufficiency will bring them success in life and relationships. But how long can we truly hide from the One who knows us inside and out? The truth is that embracing spiritual nakedness is the first step in aligning ourselves with God's plan for true success both in relationships and in life itself. It teaches us that openness to God and to each other is the key to genuine connection, healing, and growth.

In embracing spiritual nakedness, we are not just enhancing our relationships with others but aligning our lives with God's divine purpose. We must continually seek to live in a state of vulnerability before God, surrendering our pride, control, and fears to Him. Only by doing this can we truly experience the fullness of the love and peace that God intends for us. When we are open to His guidance, we become more effective in our relationships and more equipped to handle life's challenges. The world teaches us to be self-reliant and to guard ourselves against vulnerability, but God's Word teaches the opposite. Proverbs 3:5-6 (NLT) reminds us: *"Trust in the Lord with all your heart; do not depend on your own understanding. Seek his will in all you do, and he will show you which path to take."* By living with spiritual nakedness, we teach future generations the importance of humility, transparency, and trust in God. This lesson will guide them in navigating relationships with openness, allowing them to experience the true success that comes from living in harmony with God's will.

NOTE THESE

Unity with God and others requires openness: Spiritual nakedness symbolizes complete transparency and alignment with God's purpose.

Surrendering to God's will transforms us: Removing personal distractions allows God to shape us into His image.

True success comes from humility and vulnerability: Spiritual nakedness fosters deeper relationships and alignment with God's plan.

Shame and pride block divine connection: Hiding from God weakens our spiritual and relational bonds.

Living in spiritual openness teaches future generations: Trusting God with our hearts sets an example of faith, love, and unity.

Conclusion

As we reach the end of *They Were Naked: The Language of Marital Unity*, I trust that the journey through the chapters has illuminated the true significance of nakedness both physical and spiritual and how it shapes our relationship with God, others, and ourselves. The biblical account of Adam and Eve's original nakedness was not merely about their bodies being exposed, but a reflection of the purity, vulnerability, and intimacy they shared with God in a state of perfect harmony. This state of openness, unmarred by shame or guilt, invites us to reflect on the condition of our own hearts and how we approach our Creator and each other. Through the exploration of these deeper meanings, we come to understand that nakedness, in its most profound sense, is an invitation to embrace vulnerability before God and to live in transparency and purity.

In this book, we have examined how spiritual nakedness is not something to be feared but rather something to be sought a state of complete surrender, openness, and humility before God. Just as the beloved in the Song of Solomon expresses her longing for intimacy, we too are called to desire and experience a deeper connection with God and those we love. Whether it is in our marriages, friendships, or personal walk with God, we must be willing to be open, honest, and unafraid to stand before Him, acknowledging our weaknesses and imperfections. As we shed our walls, masks, and distractions, we allow God to cleanse and restore us, preparing us to walk in alignment with His will.

The lessons within these pages also remind us of the importance of living with urgency and spiritual readiness. The fleeting nature of spiritual opportunities calls us to act quickly when God knocks at the door of our hearts. How often do we miss moments of divine intimacy because we are distracted, preoccupied, or unwilling to open ourselves fully? This book serves as a reminder to be constantly aware, always ready to respond to God's call, and to cherish the moments when He invites us into a deeper, more meaningful connection. Just as the beloved in the Song of Solomon did not want to miss her opportunity for union, we too should seek to be present, intentional, and attentive to God's voice in our lives.

In closing, my prayer is that the truths shared in *They Were Naked: The Language of Marital Unity* will inspire you to embrace spiritual nakedness with a new perspective one that sees it not as exposure, but as an opportunity for growth, healing, and transformation. May you allow God's love to cleanse you, purify you, and guide you in every area of your life. The power of spiritual nakedness is that it leads to a deeper relationship with God and brings a greater sense of fulfillment and purpose in our relationships. May this book serve as a constant reminder of the beauty of living in transparency before God, walking in unity with His will, and experiencing the fullness of His love and grace. God bless you as you continue to embrace the transformative power of nakedness in your spiritual journey.

References

Aguas, J.J., 2020. The philosophical foundation of John Paul II's notions of marriage and unity of man and woman in his Theology of the Body. *Philippiniana Sacra*, 55(164), p.58.

Alaimo, S., 2010. The naked word: The trans-corporeal ethics of the protesting body. *Women & Performance: a journal of feminist theory*, 20(1), pp.15-36.

Armstrong, K., 2010. *The case for God*. Anchor.

Bauks, M., 2012. Knowledge, Nakedness, and Shame in the Primeval History of the Hebrew Bible and in Several Texts from the Judean Desert. *The Hebrew Bible in the Light of the Dead Sea scrolls*, pp.172-85.

Bauks, M., 2012. Knowledge, Nakedness, and Shame in the Primeval History of the Hebrew Bible and in Several Texts from the Judean Desert. *The Hebrew Bible in the Light of the Dead Sea scrolls*, pp.172-85.

Benner, D.G., 2015. *Surrender to love: Discovering the heart of Christian spirituality*. InterVarsity Press.

Benner, D.G., 2015. *The gift of being yourself: The sacred call to self-discovery*. InterVarsity Press.

Burke, J., 2013. Nakedness and other peoples: Rethinking the italian renaissance nude. *Art History*, 36(4), pp.714-739.

Campbell, J. and Campbell, J., 1969. *The masks of God: Primitive mythology* (p. 278). New York: Viking Press.

Candeub, A., 2018. Nakedness and publicity. *Iowa L. Rev.*, 104, p.1747.

Clark, K. and Beal, B., 2019. *Sex, Purity, and the Longings of a Girl's Heart: Discovering the Beauty and Freedom of God-Defined Sexuality.* Baker Books.

Clark, K., 2023. *The nude: A study in ideal form* (Vol. 2). Princeton University Press.

Clines, D.A., 1968. The image of God in man. *Tyndale Bulletin*, *19*(1), pp.53-103.

Clines, D.J., 1976. Theme in Genesis 1-11. *The catholic biblical quarterly*, pp.483-507.

De Clercq, E., 2011. The Vulnerability of the Body: A Daring Christian Approach to Nakedness. *Bijdragen*, *72*(2), pp.183-200.

Dickinson, E., 2011. " Must we dance naked?": Art, Beauty, and Law in Munich and Paris, 1911-1913. *Journal of the History of Sexuality*, *20*(1), pp.95-131.

Donohue, D.J., 2015. Sacred Nakedness Narraphor: The Untold Story of Shame & Glory.

Donohue, D.J., 2015. Sacred Nakedness Narraphor: The Untold Story of Shame & Glory.

Ehrlich, J.S., 2014. *Regulating desire: From the virtuous maiden to the purity princess.* State University of New York Press.

Erbele-Küster, D., 2011. Gender and Cult: "Pure" and "Impure" as Gender-relevant Categories'. *Torah: The Bible and the Women*, *1*, pp.375-406.

Gilroy-Ware, C., 2013. *Marmorealities: Classical Nakedness In British Sculpture And Historical Painting 1798-1840* (Doctoral Dissertation, University Of York).

Górnicka, B., 2016. *Nakedness, shame, and embarrassment: A long-term sociological perspective* (Vol. 12). Springer.

Górnicka, B., 2016. *Nakedness, shame, and embarrassment: A long-term sociological perspective* (Vol. 12). Springer.

REFERENCES

Greenblatt, S., 2017. *The rise and fall of Adam and Eve: the story that created us.* WW Norton & Company.

Gushee, D.P., 2013. *The sacredness of human life: why an ancient biblical vision is key to the world's future.* Wm. B. Eerdmans Publishing.

Gushee, D.P., 2013. *The sacredness of human life: why an ancient biblical vision is key to the world's future.* Wm. B. Eerdmans Publishing.

Haddad, K.C., 2014. *Worship the First-Century Way* (Vol. 2). Northern Lights Publishing House.

Hanley, R.C., 2019. The Use of Nakedness Imagery as Theological Language in the Old Testament.

Hanley, R.C., 2019. The Use of Nakedness Imagery as Theological Language in the Old Testament.

Henderson, A., 2021. Falsely Identifying Original Sin and Pure Nature: Christological Implications. *New blackfriars, 102*(1100), pp.472-485.

Jakes, T.D., 2011. *Naked and not ashamed: We've been afraid to reveal what God longs to Heal.* Destiny Image Publishers.

Käll, L.F., 2010. Fashioned in nakedness, sculptured, and caused to be born: Bodies in light of the Sartrean gaze. *Continental philosophy review, 43,* pp.61-81.

Käll, L.F., 2010. Fashioned in nakedness, sculptured, and caused to be born: Bodies in light of the Sartrean gaze. *Continental philosophy review, 43,* pp.61-81.

Kass, L., 2003. *The beginning of wisdom: Reading Genesis.* Simon and Schuster.

Kilner, J.F., 2015. *Dignity and destiny: Humanity in the image of God.* Wm. B. Eerdmans Publishing.

Kilner, J.F., 2015. *Dignity and destiny: Humanity in the image of God.* Wm. B. Eerdmans Publishing.

Lé, D., 2012. *The naked Christ: An atonement model for a body-obsessed culture* (Vol. 7). Wipf and Stock Publishers.

Letellier, R.I., 2016. *Creation, Sin and Reconciliation: Reading Primordial and Patriarchal Narrative in the Book of Genesis*. Cambridge Scholars Publishing.

Levinas, E., 1998. *Of God who comes to mind*. Stanford University Press.

Levine, P., 2013. Naked Truths: Bodies, Knowledge, and the Erotics of Colonial Power. *Journal of British Studies, 52*(1), pp.5-25.

Magonet, J., 1992. The themes of Génesis 2-3. *A walk in the garden: Biblical, iconographical and literary images of Eden, 136*, p.39.

Mathebula, M., 2022. Nakedness as decolonial praxis. *Body & Society, 28*(3), pp.3-29.

McLaren, B.D., 2011. *Naked spirituality*. Hachette UK.

Miles, M.R., 2006. *Carnal knowing: Female nakedness and religious meaning in the Christian west*. Wipf and Stock Publishers.

Ostriker, A., 1994. *The nakedness of the fathers: Biblical visions and revisions*. Rutgers University Press.

Pagels, E., 2011. *Adam, Eve, and the serpent: Sex and politics in early Christianity*. Vintage.

Panda, A., 2024. Can nakedness speak? Re-thinking Mahasweta Devi's narratives of insurgent victimhood in the era of naked protests. *Asian Journal of Women's Studies, 30*(4), pp.285-311.

Pinnock, C.H., Rice, R., Sanders, J., Hasker, W. and Basinger, D., 2010. *The openness of God: A biblical challenge to the traditional understanding of God*. InterVarsity Press.

Pinnock, C.H., Rice, R., Sanders, J., Hasker, W. and Basinger, D., 2010. *The openness of God: A biblical challenge to the traditional understanding of God*. InterVarsity Press.

Routledge, A., 2014. *'Dress and undress thy soul': nakedness and theology in early modern literature and culture* (Doctoral dissertation, University of Birmingham).

Rüterswörden, U., 2013. Purity conceptions in Deuteronomy. In *Purity and the Forming of Religious Traditions in the Ancient Mediterranean World and Ancient Judaism* (pp. 413-428). Brill.

Schreiner, T.R., 2013. *The king in his beauty: a biblical theology of the Old and New Testaments*. Baker Books.

Scott, M.S., 2012. *Journey back to God: Origen on the problem of evil*. Oxford University Press.

Scott, S. and Lambert, H. eds., 2012. *Counseling the Hard Cases: True Stories Illustrating the Sufficiency of God's Resources in Scripture*. B&H Publishing Group.

Senn, F.C., 2016. Embodied Liturgy: Lessons in Christian Ritual. Augsburg Fortress Publishers.

Sheldon, J., Listening to the Conversations of Biblical Text.

Skousen, W.C., 2014. *The Naked Communist: Exposing Communism and Restoring Freedom* (Vol. 1). Izzard Ink.

Snoeberger, M.A., 2017. Nakedness & Coverings in Genesis 3: What They are and Why it Matters. *Detroit Baptist Seminary Journal*, 22, pp.21-33.

Tembo, K.D., 2022. Being-in-Danger: Being, Precarity, and Potential– Theoretical Speculations on the Palimpsestic Naked Body. *Corpus Mundi*, *3*(1 (9)), pp.15-30.

The Holy Bible: King James Version. Electronic Edition of the 1900 Authorized Version. Bellingham, WA: Logos Research Systems, Inc., 2009. Print.

The New International Version. Grand Rapids, MI: Zondervan, 2011. Print.

The New King James Version. Nashville: Thomas Nelson, 1982. Print.

Tolstoy, L., 2022. *The kingdom of God is within you.* DigiCat.

Tozer, A.W., 2010. *The Purpose of Man: Designed to Worship.* ReadHowYouWant.com.

Vernon, K., 2024. *Outrageous and Outdated: When Purity Culture Shapes Evangelical Beliefs about Women and Sexuality* (Doctoral dissertation).

Vorster, N., 2011. *Created in the image of God: Understanding God's relationship with humanity* (Vol. 173). Wipf and Stock Publishers.

Weiss, D., 2013. *Clean: A proven plan for men committed to sexual integrity.* Thomas Nelson.

Westerlund, F., 2023. Exposed: On Shame and Nakedness. *Philosophia, 51*(4), pp.2195-2223.

Yarwood, A., 1980. *Naked and Afraid. A Study of Genesis III, Verse 7 and Its Interpretation* (Doctoral dissertation).

Zellentin, H.M., 2019. Gentile purity law from the Bible to the Qur'an: The case of sexual purity and illicit intercourse. In *The Qur'an's Reformation of Judaism and Christianity* (pp. 115-215). Routledge.

Zornberg, A.G., 2011. *The beginning of desire: Reflections on Genesis.* Schocken.

Bible References

Genesis 2:25
Genesis 3:7
Genesis 3:10
Ezekiel 16:8
Revelation 3:18
Matthew 27:28
Romans 8:1
Genesis 3:21
Romans 13:14
Genesis 3:8
Psalm 139:23-24
Psalm 139:1-4
1 John 1:9
Romans 8:1
Hebrews 4:16
Genesis 2:25
Romans 12:2
2 Corinthians 5:21
Revelation 21:3-4
2 Corinthians 5:21

Genesis 1:27
Revelation 21:3-4
Psalm 139:14
2 Corinthians 5:17
Matthew 5:14-16
Genesis 2:23
Genesis 2:25
Proverbs 27:5
Hebrews 4:13
Genesis 3:7-12
Genesis 2:25
1 John 1:9
Romans 8:1
Genesis 2:25
Psalm 51:10
Matthew 6:33
2 Corinthians 12:9
Proverbs 10:9
Hebrews 4:13
Matthew 5:8

1 Samuel 18:3-4
John 21:15-19
Ruth 3:9-11
Genesis 3:9-10
Psalm 139:23-24
Ecclesiastes 5:15
Philippians 2:7
Job 1:21
Genesis 2:25
James 5:16
Hebrews 4:13
Matthew 6:33
Hebrews 4:13
Matthew 11:28-29
Psalm 34:18
Job 1:21
Matthew 6:19-20
Matthew 16:26
Luke 12:16-21
Luke 12:21

Matthew 6:19-21	Proverbs 11:2	John 14:15
Ecclesiastes 5:16	Isaiah 29:15	Romans 12:2
Matthew 6:19-20	2 Corinthians 12:9	Matthew 23:26
Colossians 3:1-2	Hebrews 12:1	Matthew 5:37
James 1:17	Romans 12:2	Matthew 23:28
Genesis 3:7	John 4:24	Proverbs 10:9
Job 1:21	Isaiah 29:13	Psalm 139:23-24
Ecclesiastes 5:15	Psalm 51:17	Matthew 15:7-9
Genesis 3:6-7	John 4:23-24	Matthew 15:7-9
Romans 3:23	James 4:10	Matthew 15:9,
Luke 15:17-24).	Romans 12:1	John 8:31-32
Exodus 33:14	John 14:6	Romans 12:2
1 Timothy 6:7	John 4:23-24	Matthew 6:33
Job 1:21	Romans 12:1	Proverbs 23:26
Psalm 24:1	Matthew 5:8	Matthew 16:24-25
Job 2:10	Psalm 51:10	John 4:23-24,
Proverbs 3:5-6	John 14:15	Matthew 15:8-9
Ecclesiastes 5:19	Ezekiel 33:31	2 Corinthians 13:5
1 Timothy 6:17-18	Matthew 15:7-9	Matthew 7:16
1 Samuel 16:7	John 4:24	Matthew 15:8
Micah 6:8	Hebrews 4:13	Galatians 6:4
Hebrews 4:13	Psalm 139:23-24	Luke 18:9-14
Isaiah 29:13	Psalm 51:17	Luke 18:13
1 Timothy 2:9-10	Ezekiel 33:3	Galatians 6:5
Psalm 51:10	Matthew 15:7-9	Psalm 139:1-2
Matthew 5:8	James 1:22	2 Corinthians 12:9
Hebrews 4:13	Psalm 139:23-24	James 4:8
Isaiah 29:13	Hebrews 4:12	Psalm 139:7-10
Matthew 15:8	Ezekiel 33:31	Mark 10:50
Luke 18:10-14	Matthew 15:7-9	Mark 10:51
1 Samuel 16:7	Ezekiel 36:26	Mark 10:52

BIBLE REFERENCES

Ephesians 4:22-24
1 Timothy 6:6-8
Ecclesiastes 5:19
Philippians 4:11-12
Matthew 6:33
Ephesians 5:31
Psalm 42:1-2
Genesis 2:23
Matthew 5:6
John 15:5
Galatians 5:22-23
Psalm 63:1
John 8:32
Proverbs 2:11
Hebrews 5:14
Ecclesiastes 3:1
Colossians 3:14
James 4:10
Ephesians 5:8
Ephesians 5:31
Philippians 2:3-4
Genesis 3:6
Matthew 19:5
Ephesians 5:25
Genesis 2:24
Ephesians 5:25
Ephesians 5:33
Ephesians 4:32
2 Corinthians 5:18
Romans 12:10

Proverbs 11:14
Galatians 6:2
Proverbs 15:22
Colossians 3:13
James 4:10
Matthew 18:21-22
Proverbs 16:3
Matthew 19:6
1 Corinthians 13:7
James 1:3-4
Romans 8:28
1 Corinthians 13:3
Ecclesiastes 4:9-10
1 Corinthians 13:8
Matthew 6:19-21
Colossians 3:13
Hebrews 4:13
2 Corinthians 12:9
Proverbs 3:5-6
Revelation 3:20
Matthew 6:33
Philippians 4:13
Proverbs 3:5-6,
Genesis 2:25,
In Ephesians 4:2-3
Philippians 4:13
Song of Solomon 5:1-2
Revelation 3:20
Ephesians 5:25-27
Genesis 3:10

Proverbs 3:5-6
Philippians 4:13
Corinthians 12:9
James 5:16
Song of Solomon 5:2
Revelation 3:20
Hebrews 4:13
Philippians 2:7-8
Song of Solomon 5:2
John 13:8
James 4:8
Matthew 13:22
Proverbs 3:5-6
1 John 4:18
Matthew 26:41
James 4:4
Song of Solomon 5:6
Revelation 3:20
2 Corinthians 6:2
Matthew 25:13
Psalm 51:17
Ephesians 5:21-25
John 15:5
Romans 12:2
Ephesians 4:3-6
John 13:5
Genesis 2:25
Proverbs 3:5-6
Ephesians 5:21
Ecclesiastes 4:9-10

Other Books
by the Author

  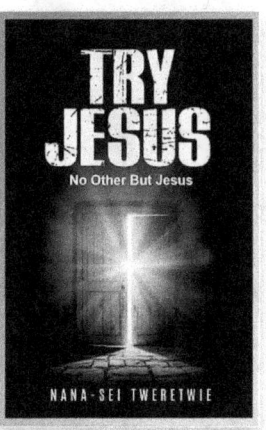

And many more...

Author's Profile

Nana-Sei Tweretwie is a seasoned minister with a legacy of impactful service in spreading the gospel. As the Lead Pastor and Founder of Miracle Temple Assemblies of God in Milton Keynes, UK, he has established and nurtured congregations in both the UK and Ghana. Beyond the pulpit, he serves as a marriage and family counsellor, teaches life coaching and leadership and contributes to missionary leadership across global organizations.

With an MA in Biblical Studies in the UK, Reverend Tweretwie tirelessly shares the love of Jesus Christ across North America, Asia, Europe, and Africa. He is married to Rev. Mrs. Yvonne Tweretwie. Together, they are blessed with five children and three grandchildren. They are all engaged in the work of the Lord and inspire others to deepen their walk with God.

www.ingramcontent.com/pod-product-compliance
Lightning Source LLC
Chambersburg PA
CBHW071202070526
44584CB00019B/2891